Contents

Links to Abacus weekly plans

This information is for teachers who want to see how the Mastery Checkpoints are planned into the Abacus maths programme.

Autumn term 1		
Week 1	Checkpoint 1	Place value
Week 1	Checkpoint 2	Mental and written addition
Week 4	Checkpoint 3	The 24-hour clock
Autumn term 2		
Week 6	Checkpoint 4	Factors
Week 7	Checkpoint 5	Mental and written division
Week 8	Checkpoint 6	Angles
Week 9	Checkpoint 7	Ordering numbers with two decimal places
Week 9	Checkpoint 8	Equivalent fractions
Week 10	Checkpoint 9	Mental and written subtraction
Week 10	Checkpoint 10	Mental and written multiplication
Spring term 1		
Week 11	Checkpoint 11	Place value in 6-digit numbers
Week 11	Checkpoint 12	Numbers with two decimal places
Week 12	Checkpoint 13	Solving word problems involving measures
Week 12	Checkpoint 14	Mental addition and subtraction of large numbers
Week 13	Checkpoint 15	Factors, primes, squares and mental multiplication and division
Week 14	Checkpoint 16	Triangles, including their angles
Week 14	Checkpoint 17	Converting measures
Week 15	Checkpoint 18	Adding and subtracting decimals
Spring term 2		
Week 16	Checkpoint 19	Short division
Week 17	Checkpoint 20	Finding fractions of amounts
Week 17	Checkpoint 21	Multiplying pairs of 2-digit numbers and 3-digit numbers by 1-digit numbers
Week 18	Checkpoint 22	Properties of polygons
Week 19	Checkpoint 23	Improper fractions, mixed numbers and equivalent fractions
Week 20	Checkpoint 24	Subtracting 4-digit numbers and adding more than two numbers
Summer term 1		
Week 21	Checkpoint 25	Solving and checking word problems
Week 22	Checkpoint 26	Multiplying proper fractions
Week 22	Checkpoint 27	Short multiplication methods
Week 23	Checkpoint 28	Working with 3-place decimals
Week 23	Checkpoint 29	Solving problems with negative numbers
Week 24	Checkpoint 30	Working with coordinates in the first two quadrants
Week 24	Checkpoint 31	Drawing 2D shapes and identifying 3D shapes from nets
Week 25	Checkpoint 32	Using column methods to solve and check addition and subtraction problems
Summer term 2		
Week 26	Checkpoint 33	Comparing, adding and subtracting fractions
Week 27	Checkpoint 34	Short division
Week 27	Checkpoint 35	Multiplying 3-digit and 4-digit numbers by teens numbers
Week 28	Checkpoint 36	Finding areas and perimeters
Week 28	Checkpoint 37	Volume and capacity
Week 29	Checkpoint 38	Fractions, decimals and percentages
Week 30	Checkpoint 39	Reading line graphs
Week 30	Checkpoint 40	Solving problems involving scaling or rate

How to use this book

Mastery Checkpoints

The Mastery Checkpoints give you a chance to show how much you have learned about a key maths skill, straight after you have learned about it in lessons.

Each Checkpoint starts with a few questions for everyone to try. These are followed by some more in-depth questions in the Champions' Challenge section.

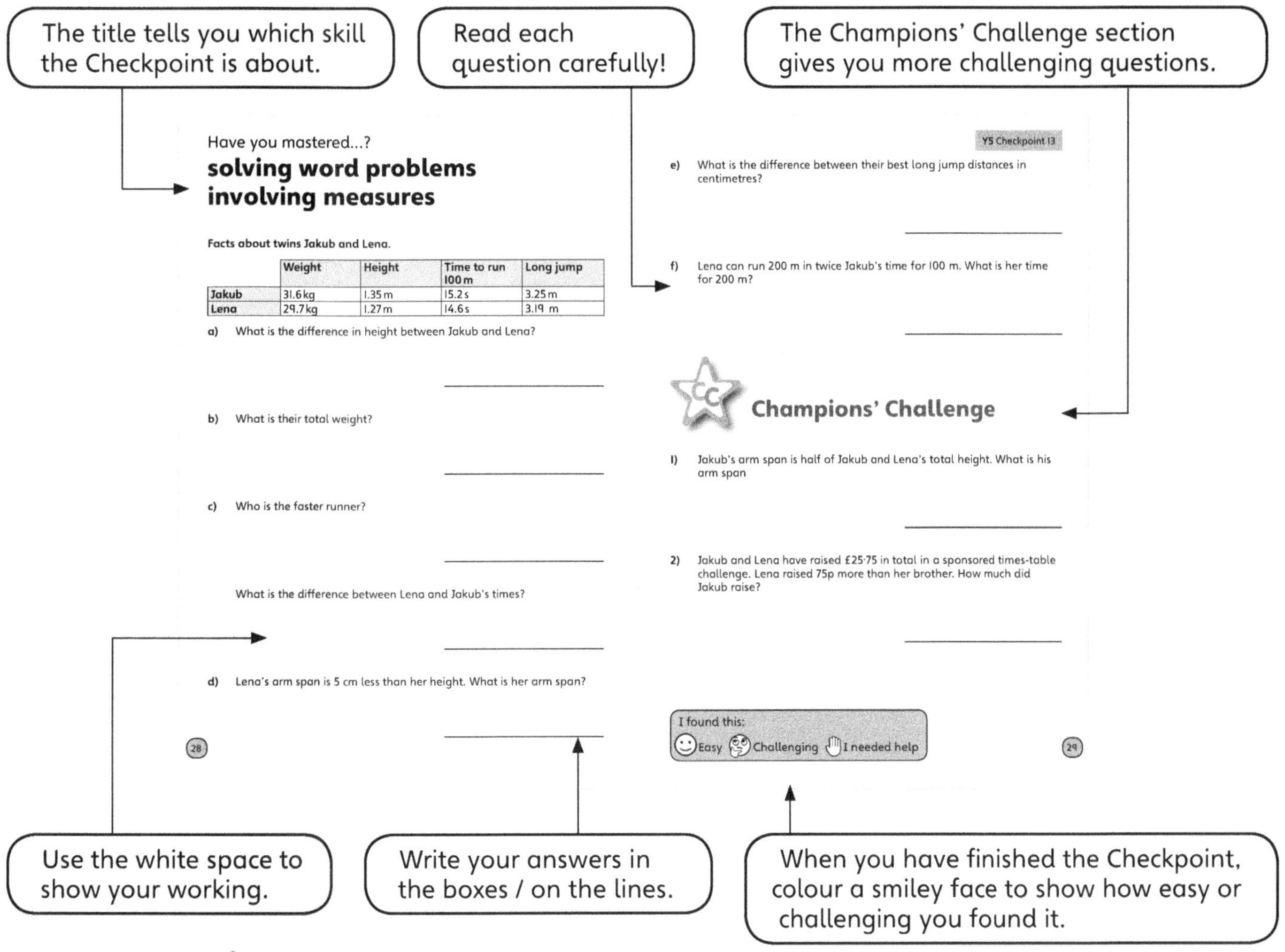

My Learning

On pages 88–93 you will find opportunities for you to reflect on your own learning: for example, how you and your classmates have helped each other to learn, what important questions you have asked, and what connections you have found between different areas of maths. Your teacher will tell you when to complete each of these pages.

My Mastery

On pages 94–99 you will find tables that list the Checkpoint skills, and give you a chance to re-assess how confident you feel about each of them later in the year. Your teacher will tell you when to complete these self-assessments, for example, at the end of each half-term.

Have you mastered...?

place value

a) Fill the boxes with the digits 0 to 9 to make a true inequality statement:

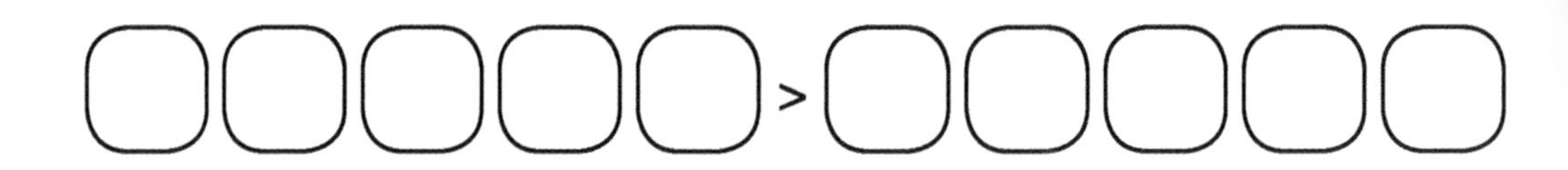

b) Write three different numbers where the digit 5 is worth 5000. Then write them in order from smallest to largest.

c) Write < or > between each pair of numbers.

23400 ☐ 24300   39989 ☐ 40100   90000 ☐ 89990

Champions' Challenge

1) Write a pair of numbers with a difference of sixty thousand, four hundred and two.

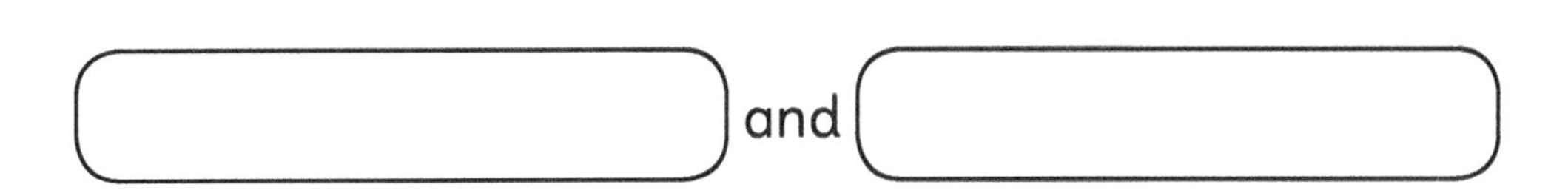

2) Write a number in the box to make this statement true:

37 643 < 38 429 − ☐

I found this:

Have you mastered...?

mental and written addition

Work out these additions.

Think carefully about which method to use each time. Use at least two different methods.

a) 7825 + 473

b) 3782 + 1999

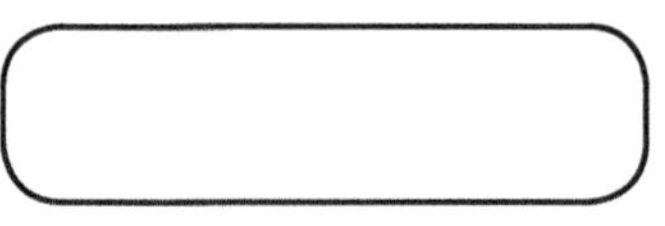

c) 6234 + 302

d) 8576 + 5247

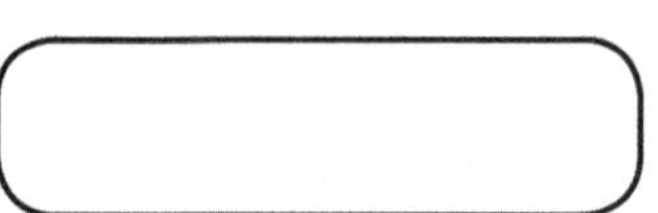

Champions' Challenge

Write two additions with answers between 10 000 and 20 000, where there are no zeros in any of the numbers!

1) Your first addition should be one that you would work out mentally.

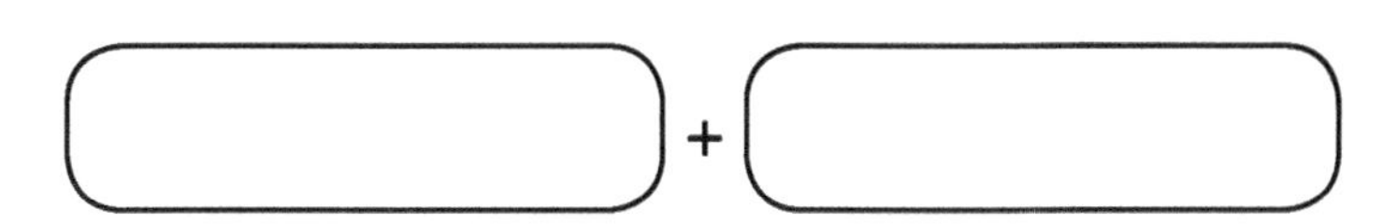

2) Your second addition should be one that you would answer using column addition.

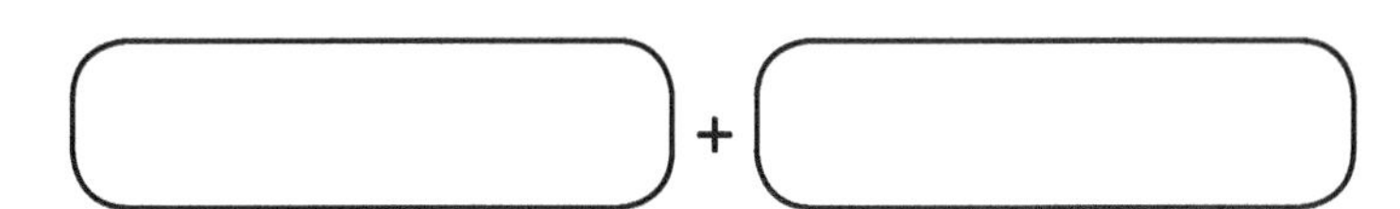

I found this:

 Easy  Challenging  I needed help

Have you mastered...?

the 24-hour clock

a) What time does the 09:46 train from Mertown get into Hiattle? Draw an analogue clock showing this time.

Train timetable		
Mertown	09:46	10:53
Kurtbridge	11:27	12:34
Hiattle	13:05	14:12
Pritchampton	14:39	15:46

b) Jamal is catching the train from Mertown. He wants to be in Kurtbridge before midday. Which train should he catch?

How long will it take?

c) The 10:53 from Mertown is delayed by 15 minutes. Will it still get to Pritchampton by 4pm?

Champions' Challenge

1) Do the two trains take the same amount of time to get from Mertown to Pritchampton? Convince your teacher of your answer!

2) What is the longest time between stops?

Have you mastered...?

factors

a) Find at least two numbers less than 40 which have six factors.

____

b) Find at least two numbers less than 40 which have four factors.

[ ] and [ ]

Champions' Challenge

Kurt thinks that even numbers have an even number of factors and odd numbers have an odd number of factors.

1) Find some examples which will help him to see that this is not true.

____

____

____

2) Explain how you can tell which numbers have an odd number of factors.

____

____

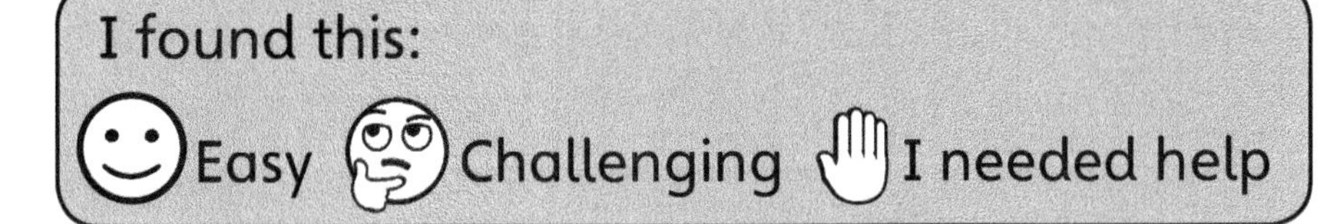

Have you mastered...?

mental and written division

a) Choose a mental or written method to work out the answers to each of these divisions.

$96 \div 4$

$480 \div 6$

$347 \div 5$

$320 \div 8$

$443 \div 7$

b) A bus route round a city centre is 9 miles. The bus travels 270 miles in one day on this route. How many loops round the city centre does the bus complete in one day?

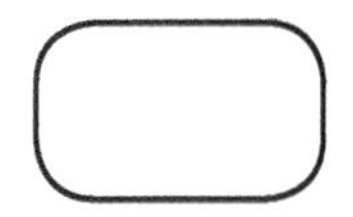

Champions' Challenge

Write two different divisions where a 3-digit number gives a remainder of 3 when you divide by 5.

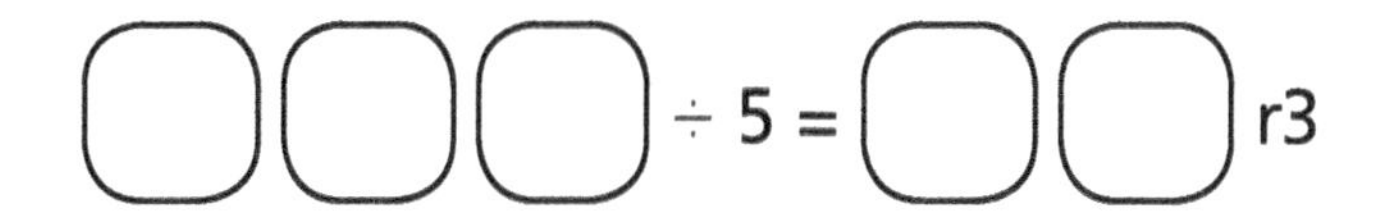

☐☐☐ ÷ 5 = ☐☐ r3

I found this:

 Easy  Challenging I needed help

Have you mastered...?

angles

a) Describe angles A, B, C, D and E. Use words such as right angle, reflex, obtuse and acute.

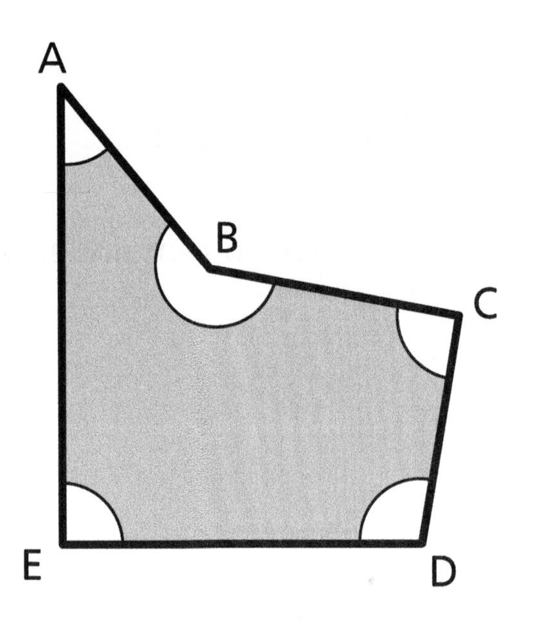

A ________________________

B ________________________

C ________________________

D ________________________

E ________________________

One angle in this shape measures 40 degrees and another measures 100 degrees.

b) Which angle do you think is 100 degrees?

____

c) Which angle do you think is 40 degrees?

____

Champions' Challenge

Sketch one diagram to show three angles with a total of 360 degrees.
One angle must be acute, one must be obtuse and the other must be
a reflex angle.

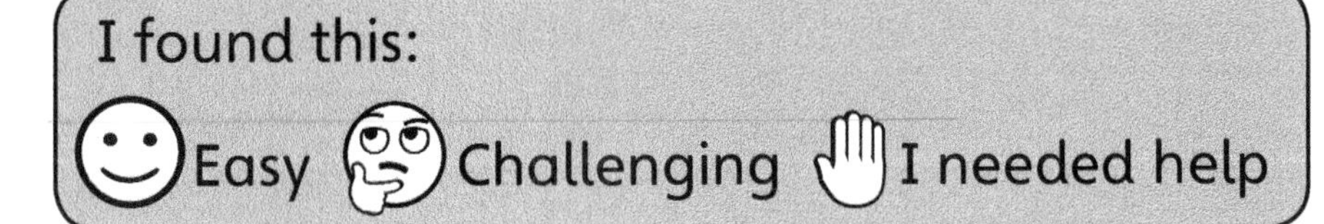

Have you mastered...?

ordering numbers with two decimal places

a) Write the correct > or < sign between each pair of numbers.

7·45 ☐ 7·28

4·32 ☐ 4·23

6·75 ☐ 6·78

2·13 ☐ 2·4

b) Write three numbers, each with two decimal places, between 4·2 and 4·3. Write them in order, smallest first.

Champions' Challenge

I am a number between 5 and 6 with three digits.

My digits add up to 10.

I am less than $5\frac{1}{4}$ but more than $5\frac{1}{5}$.

What number am I?

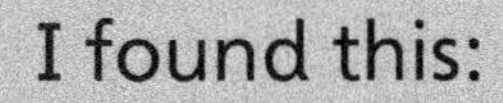

I found this:

 Easy  Challenging  I needed help

Have you mastered...?

equivalent fractions

a) Charlie says that $\frac{6}{18}$ of this grid is shaded.

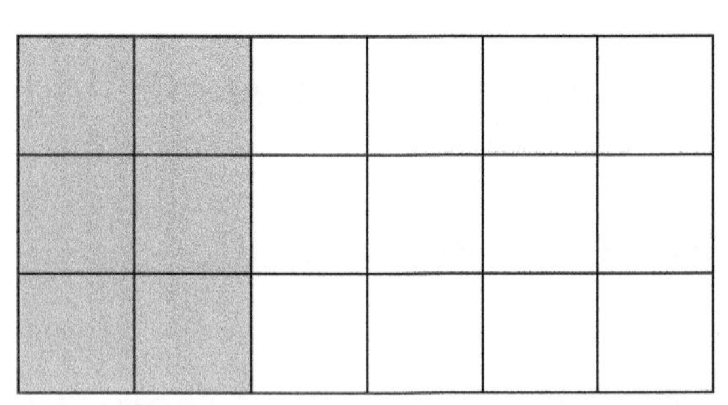

Write this fraction in the simplest way.

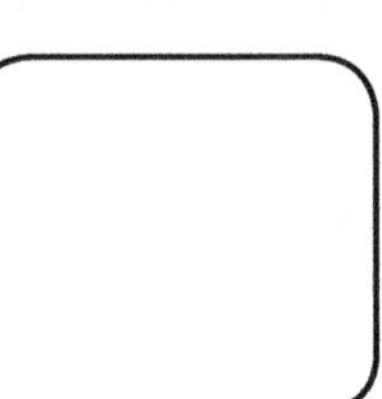

Write the fraction that is not shaded in two different ways.

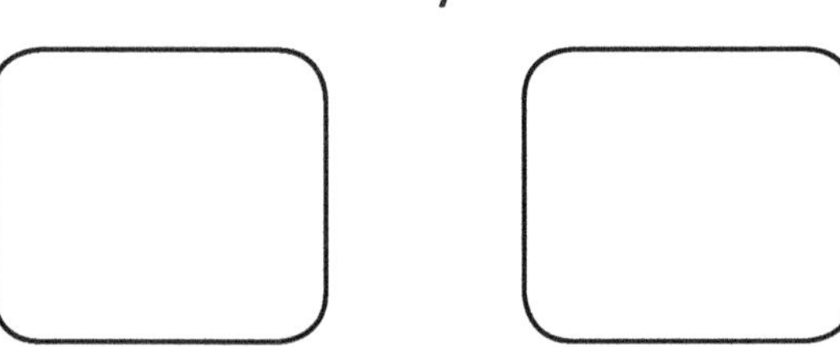

b) Spot the equivalent fractions. Write them in pairs.

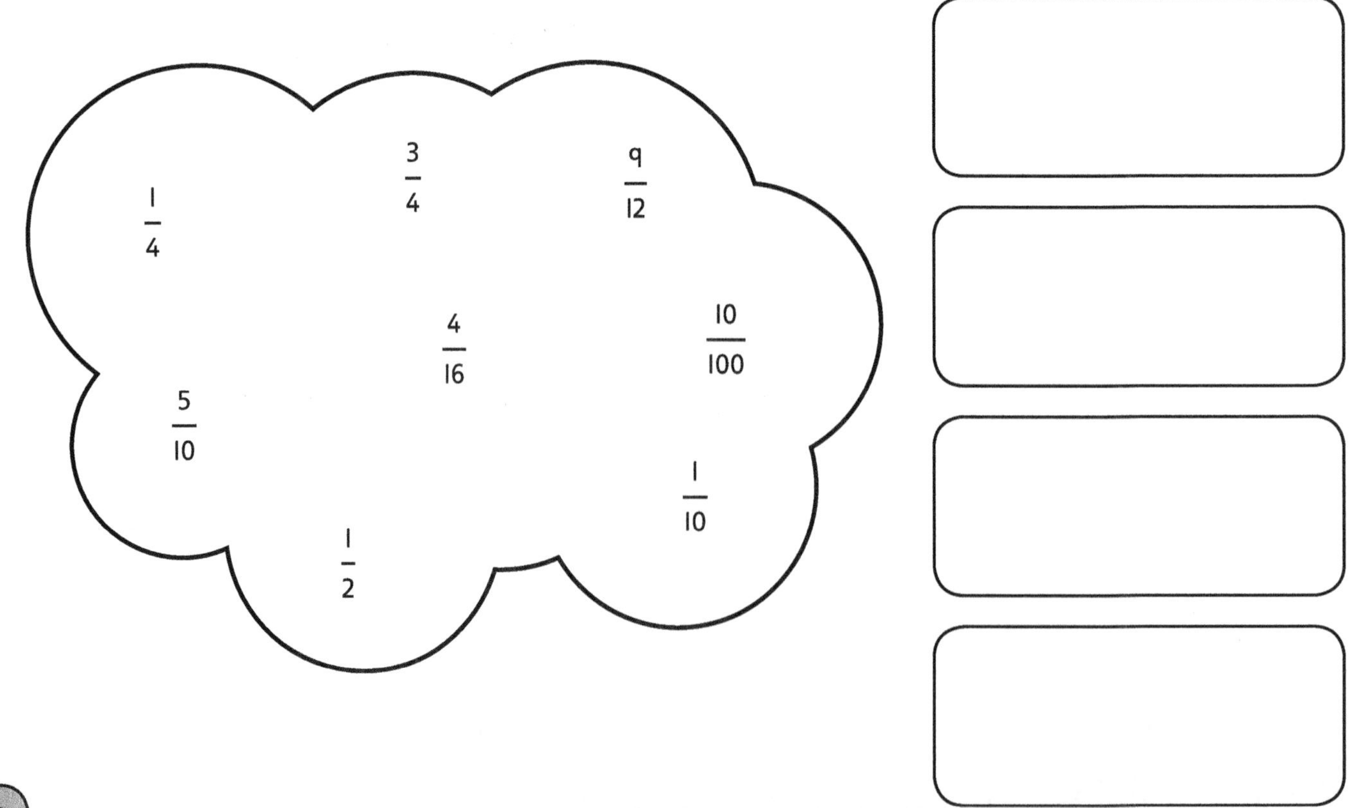

Champions' Challenge

Write at least five fractions which are equivalent to $\frac{2}{3}$.

I found this:

 Easy  Challenging  I needed help

Have you mastered...?

mental and written subtraction

Work out these subtractions. Think carefully about which method to use each time. Use at least two different methods.

a) 4003 – 2789

b) 6345 – 4278

c) 8350 – 2001

d) 8734 – 3245

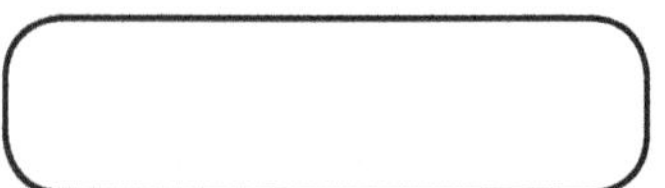

Champions' Challenge

1) Find the missing numbers:

4578 = 9623 – [ ]

8143 = [ ] + 5816

2) Write the missing digits to make this work.

[ ][ ]99 – [ ][ ]89 = 5010

I found this:

Easy Challenging I needed help

Have you mastered...?

mental and written multiplication

a) Choose a mental or written method to work out the answers to each of these multiplications:

45×3

7×642

426×2

30×60

32×67

b) A farmer has 243 chickens. If each chicken lays one egg a day, how many will they lay altogether in one week?

Champions' Challenge

1) Write three different multiplications with the answer 248.

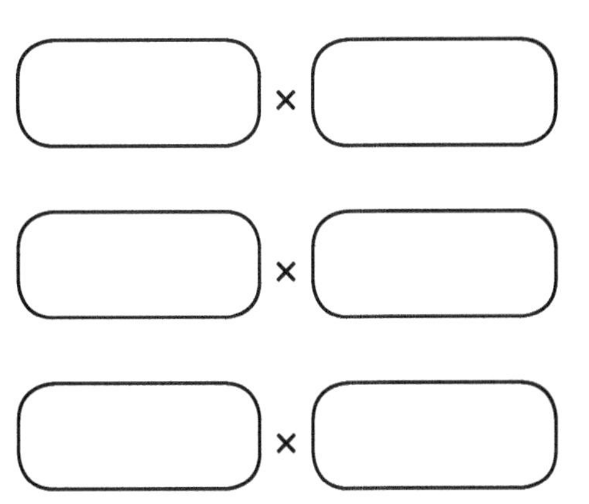

2) Write three different multiplications with the answer 3600.

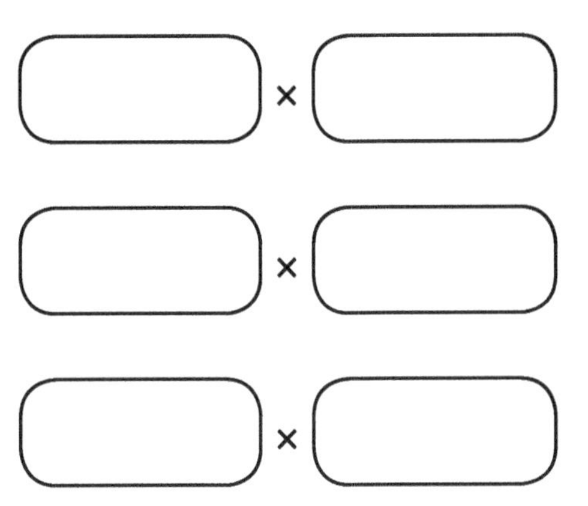

I found this:

Easy Challenging I needed help

Have you mastered...?

place value in 6-digit numbers

a) Write the number that is:

50 000 more than 247 393

6000 less than 326 487

200 000 more than 734 905

1 less than 500 000

Halfway between 425 000 and 475 000

Halfway between 320 000 and 420 000

b) Write four numbers between 250 000 and 350 000 in order, smallest first.

1. **2.**

3. **4.**

c) Write a pair of numbers between 670 000 and 700 000 with a difference of 20 000.

Champions' Challenge

1) Write the biggest 6-digit number possible where every digit is different.

Find the difference between this number and 100 000.

2) Write the smallest 6-digit number possible where every digit is different

Find the difference between this number and 100 000.

I found this:

Easy Challenging I needed help

Have you mastered...?

numbers with two decimal places

a) Complete these calculations.

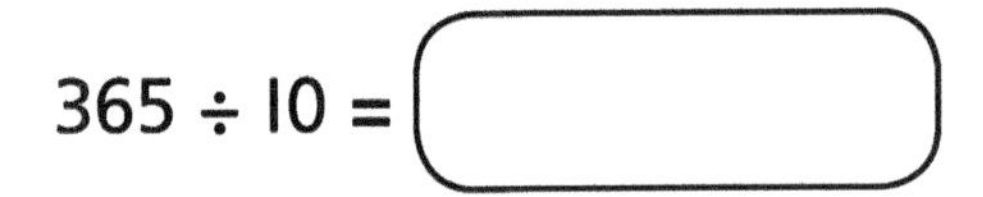

365 ÷ 10 = ☐

365 ÷ 100 = ☐

4·02 × 10 = ☐

7·5 × ☐ = 750

0·52 × ☐ = 5·2

b) Write the next three numbers in each sequence:

3·25 3·35 3·45  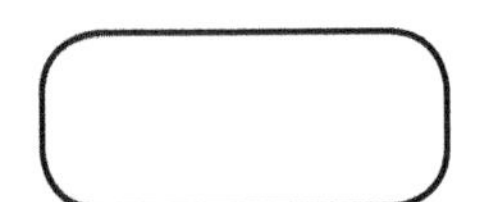

2·46 2·47 2·48  

4·42 4·32 4·22  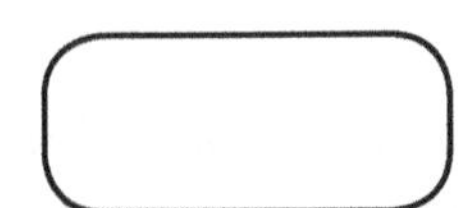

Write a number with two decimal places between 3·5 and 4·5, which:

c) rounds to 4 when rounded to the nearest whole number

d) rounds to 3·5 when rounded to the nearest tenth

e) rounds to 4·5 when rounded to the nearest tenth

Champions' Challenge

1) Think of a number that loses a digit when you divide it by 100.

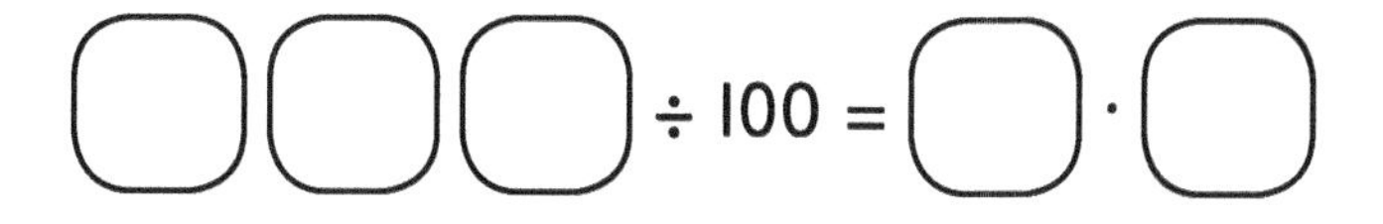

2) Think of a number that gains a digit when you divide it by 100.

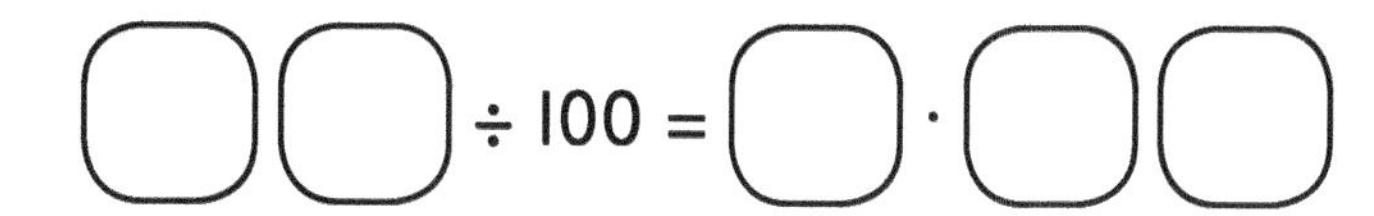

I found this:

 Easy  Challenging  I needed help

Have you mastered...?

solving word problems involving measures

Facts about twins Jakub and Lena

	Mass	Height	Time to run 100 m	Long jump
Jakub	31·6 kg	1·35 m	15·2 s	3·25 m
Lena	29·7 kg	1·27 m	14·6 s	3·19 m

a) What is the difference in height between Jakub and Lena?

____

b) What is their total mass?

____

c) Who is the faster runner?

____

What is the difference between Lena and Jakub's times?

____

d) Lena's arm span is 5 cm less than her height. What is her arm span?

____

e) What is the difference between their best long jump distances in centimetres?

____

f) Lena can run 200 m in twice Jakub's time for 100 m. What is her time for 200 m?

____

Champions' Challenge

1) Jakub's arm span is half of Jakub and Lena's total height. What is his arm span?

____

2) Jakub and Lena have raised £25·75 in total in a sponsored times-table challenge. Lena raised 75p more than her brother. How much did Jakub raise?

____

I found this:

Have you mastered...?

mental addition and subtraction of large numbers

a) Solve these additions and subtractions.

465 + 198

2421 – 199

43 261 + 5200

48 000 + 56 000

95 000 – 49 000

260 000 + 160 000

5000 – 4692

6003 – 5997

b) A skydiver free falls 1045 m before his parachute opens. This is 4055 m above the ground. What height did he jump from?

____

c) A long distance runner has run 12 050 m. She still has 2700 m to run. What is the total distance she is running today?

____

Champions' Challenge

1) Write two numbers with a total of 100 000 and a difference of 2000.

[ ] and [ ]

2) Now write two numbers with a total of 100 000 but a difference of 1998.

[ ] and [ ]

Have you mastered...?

factors, primes, squares and mental multiplication and division

a) Write a square number greater than 20.

b) Write a prime number less than 20.

c) List all the factors of 28.

____

d) Write a number with exactly four factors.

e) Solve these multiplications and divisions.

$4 \times 70 =$ ☐ $120 \times 3 =$ ☐

$9 \times 16 =$ ☐ $20 \times 20 =$ ☐

$240 \div 3 =$ ☐ $600 \div 4 =$ ☐

$147 \div 7 =$ ☐ $448 \div 4 =$ ☐

f) Work out 20 × 25. Then use this fact to work out 19 × 25, 21 × 25 and 40 × 25.

20 × 25 = ☐   19 × 25 = ☐

21 × 25 = ☐   40 × 25 = ☐

Champions' Challenge

1) Write a pair of square numbers with a difference that is a prime number.

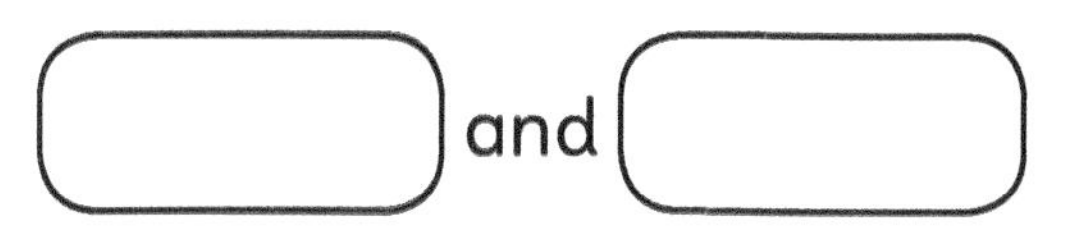

☐ and ☐

2) How many pairs of numbers like this can you write?

I found this:

 Easy  Challenging I needed help

Have you mastered...?

triangles, including their angles

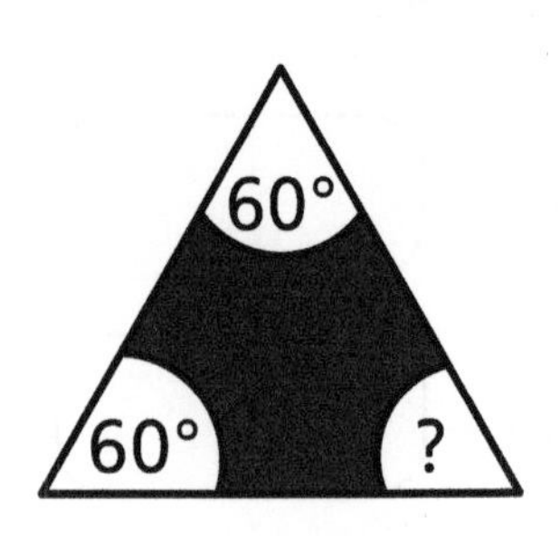

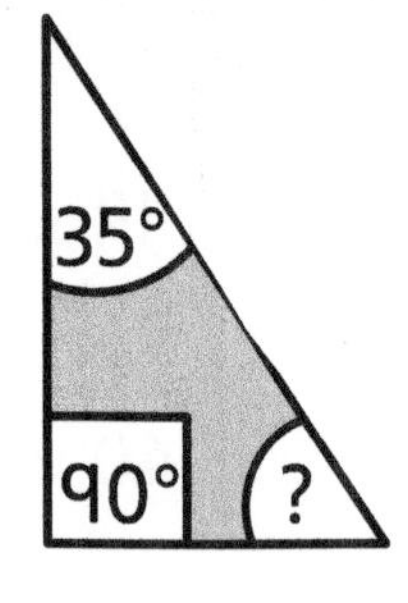

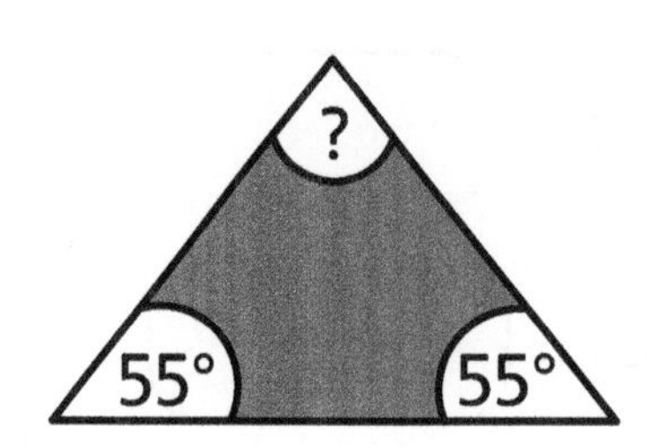

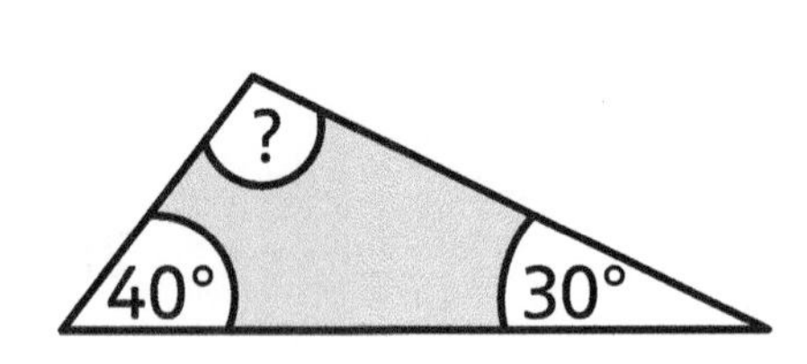

a) Work out the missing angles in:

the right-angled triangle 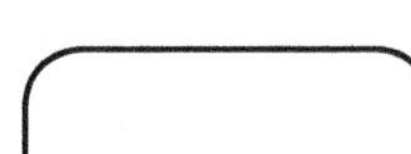

the isosceles triangle 

the equilateral triangle 

the scalene triangle 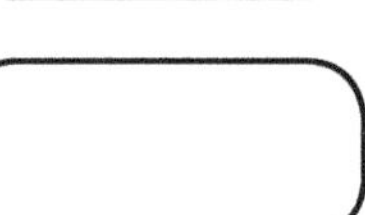

b) Complete the diagram by drawing four triangles, one by each letter.

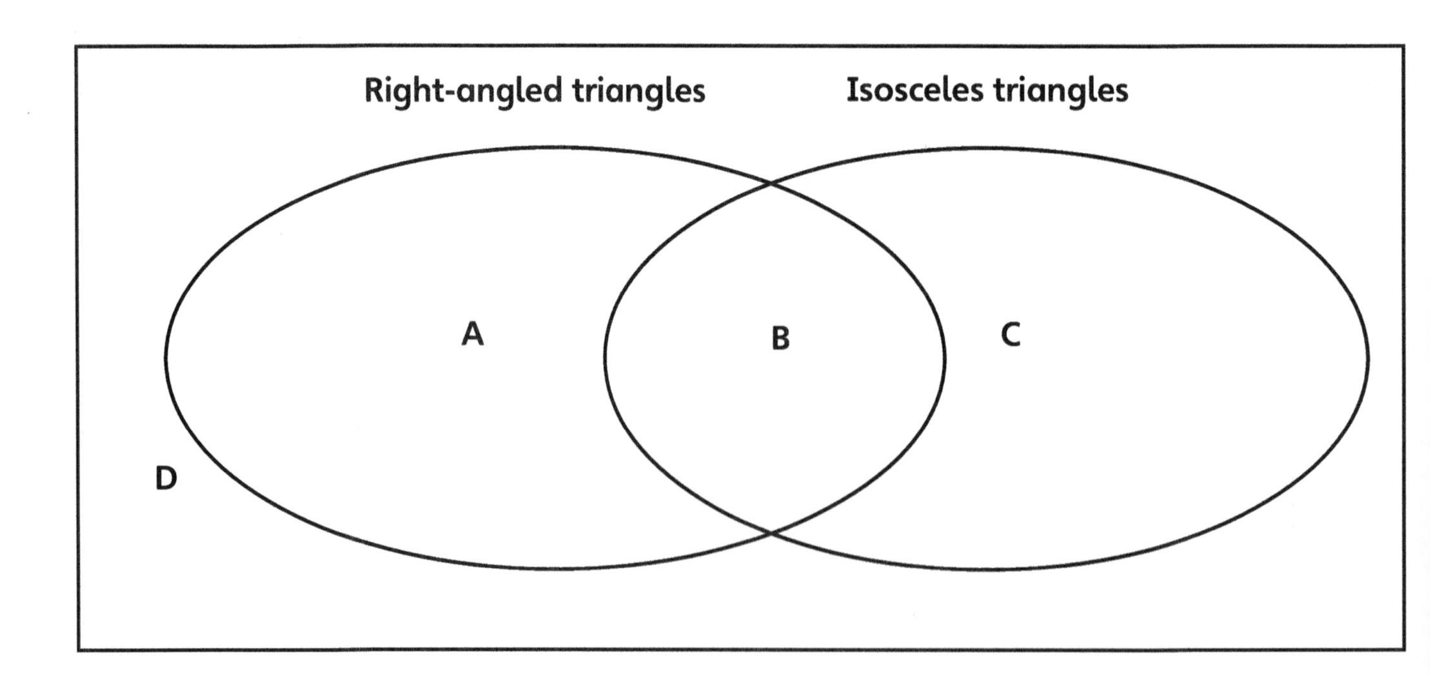

Champions' Challenge

1) This is an isosceles triangle.
Work out the missing angles.

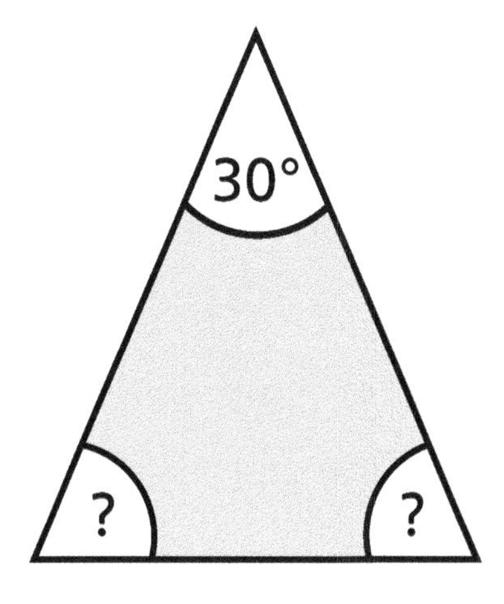

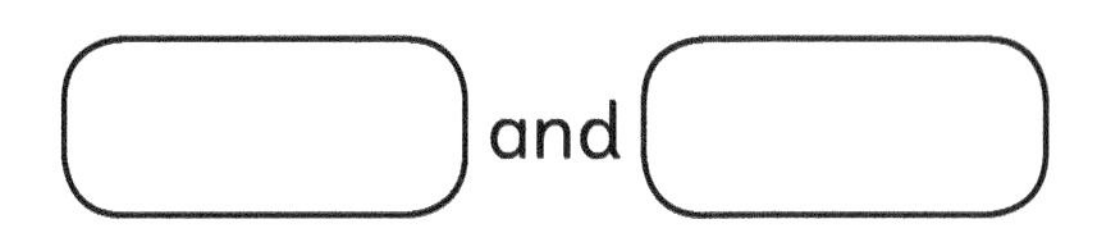

2) An equilateral triangle always has angles of 60°. Explain why.

____

____

____

____

I found this:

 Easy  Challenging  I needed help

Have you mastered...?

converting measures

a) Copy and complete.

8 kg = ☐ g

5 km = ☐ m

☐ litres = 3000 ml

1·25 m = ☐ cm

4 cm = ☐ mm

2·6 kg = ☐ g

15 km = ☐ m

3·75 litres = ☐ ml

☐ m = 400 cm

☐ cm = 16 mm

b) Write > or < between each pair of measures.

3·5 kg ☐ 2000 g

36 mm ☐ 5 cm

765 cm ☐ 6 m

2465 ml ☐ 3 litres

Champions' Challenge

1) What distance in millimetres is halfway between 32 cm and 33 cm?

____

2) What mass in grams is halfway between 2·5 kg and 2·6 kg?

____

3) Write 4 metres in millimetres.

____

4) How many millimetres are in one kilometre?

____

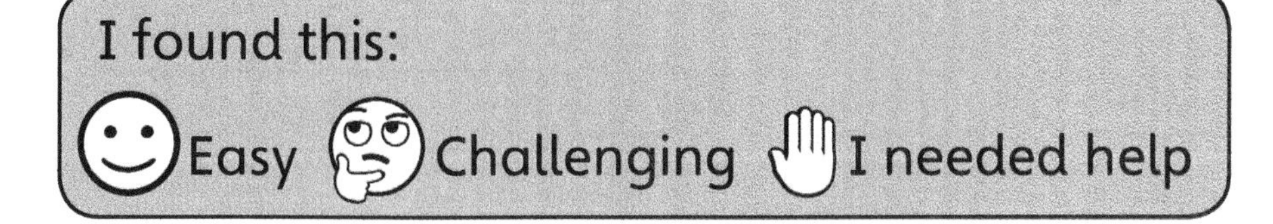

Have you mastered...?

adding and subtracting decimals

a) Choose a method to solve each of these additions and subtractions. Think carefully about when to use a written method and when it might be better to use a mental method, with or without jottings.

4·2 + 1·9

£32·67 + £12·75

5·6 kg – 1·2 kg

7 – 6·32

3·26 m – 2·89 m

34·52 + 21·86

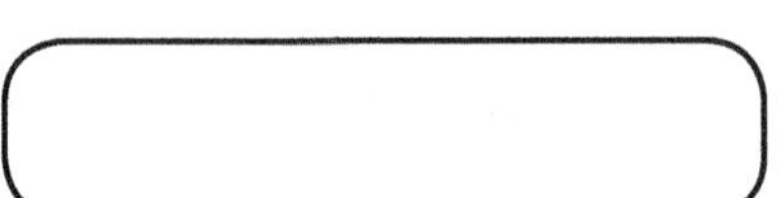

4·2 m – 3·75 m

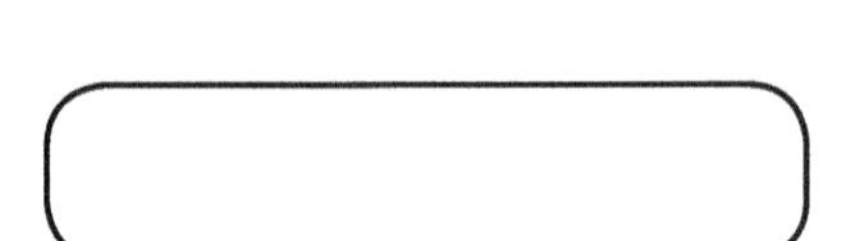

£45·75 – £9·99

b) Work out the missing digits. Remember to check your solution.

	£	5	3	·	☐	7
+	£	2	5	·	4	2
	£	7	9	·	1	9

6·2 m – 4·5 ☐ m = 1·68 m

Champions' Challenge

1) Write a pair of distances with a total of 10 metres. Each distance has three digits and all three digits are different.

☐ · ☐ ☐ m + ☐ · ☐ ☐ m = 10 m

2) Write a pair of distances with a difference of 0·5 m. Each distance has three digits and all three digits are different.

☐ · ☐ ☐ m + ☐ · ☐ ☐ m = 0·5 m

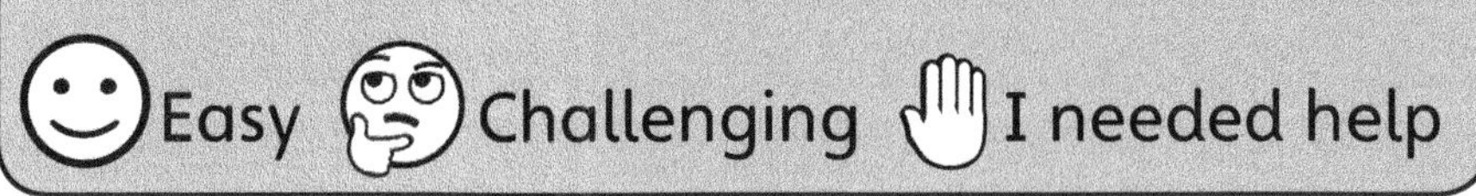

Have you mastered...?

short division

a) Work out these divisions, but look out for one which doesn't need short division!

$3\overline{)654}$

$5\overline{)527}$

$4\overline{)648}$

$8\overline{)849}$

$4\overline{)440}$

$5\overline{)786}$

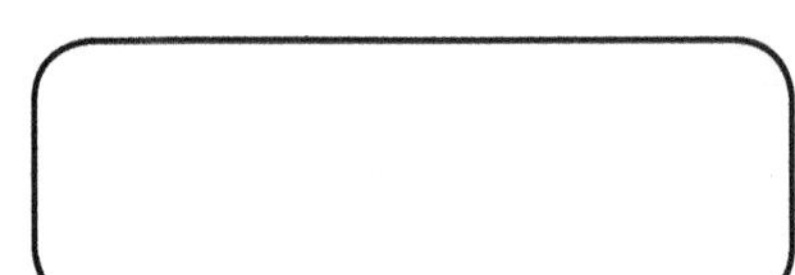

$5\overline{)163}$

$3\overline{)281}$

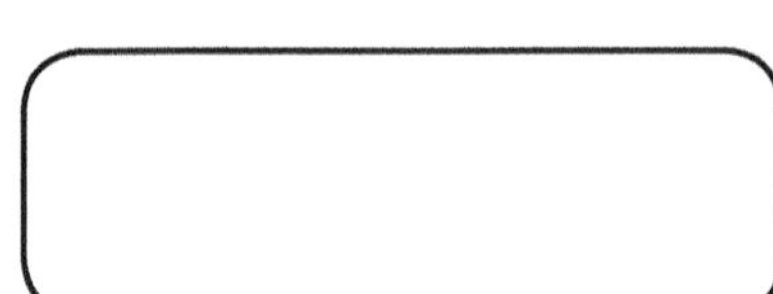

A toy manufacturer is making toy cars. There are 458 wheels.

b) If each car has 4 wheels, how many wheels will be left over?

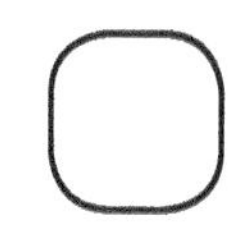

c) How many wheels would be left over if the manufacturer made trikes needing 3 wheels each?

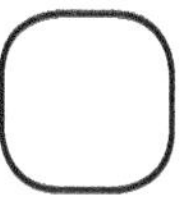

Champions' Challenge

1) Use the digits 3, 4, 5 and 6 to make two divisions like this:

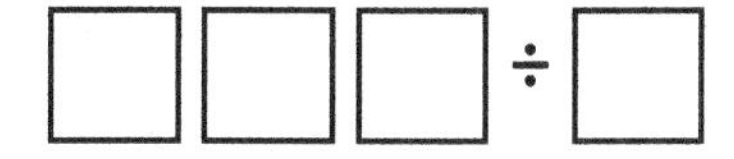

Both divisions must have a remainder of 1.

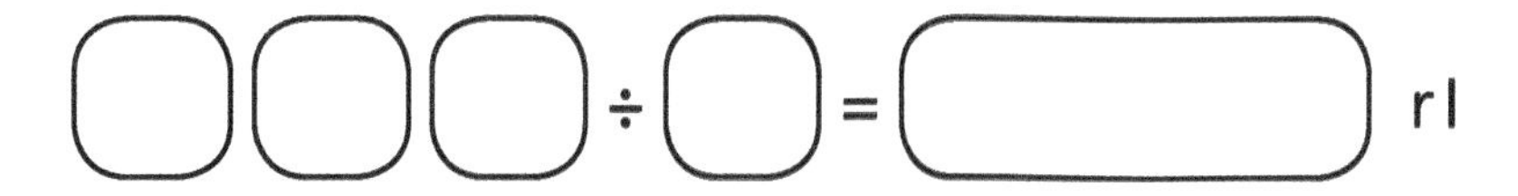

☐☐☐ ÷ ☐ = ☐ r1

I found this:

 Easy  Challenging I needed help

Have you mastered...?

finding fractions of amounts

140						
$\frac{1}{7}$	$\frac{1}{7}$	$\frac{1}{7}$	$\frac{1}{7}$	$\frac{1}{7}$	$\frac{1}{7}$	$\frac{1}{7}$

320							
$\frac{1}{8}$	$\frac{1}{8}$	$\frac{1}{8}$	$\frac{1}{8}$	$\frac{1}{8}$	$\frac{1}{8}$	$\frac{1}{8}$	$\frac{1}{8}$

192					
$\frac{1}{6}$	$\frac{1}{6}$	$\frac{1}{6}$	$\frac{1}{6}$	$\frac{1}{6}$	$\frac{1}{6}$

a) $\frac{1}{7}$ of 140 is

$\frac{3}{7}$ of 140 is

$\frac{1}{8}$ of 320 is

$\frac{5}{8}$ of 320 is

$\frac{1}{6}$ of 192 is

$\frac{5}{6}$ of 192 is

b) Dan is cycling 120 miles. He has cycled $\frac{2}{3}$ of the way. How many more miles does he have to cycle?

c) There are 365 days in a year. It rains on $\frac{2}{5}$ of them. How many days does it rain?

d) $\frac{3}{4}$ of a mystery number is 120. What is the mystery number?

Champions' Challenge

1) $\frac{5}{6}$ of ☐ is 250

2) $\frac{☐}{7}$ of 280 is 160

3) 

$\frac{5}{☐}$ of 640 is 400

I found this:

 Easy  Challenging I needed help

Have you mastered...?

multiplying pairs of 2-digit numbers and 3-digit numbers by 1-digit numbers

a) Choose pairs of numbers to multiply together to give a product between:

1500 and 2000

☐ × ☐

2000 and 3000

☐ × ☐

3500 and 4500

☐ × ☐

4500 and 5500

☐ × ☐

b) Solve these multiplications.

21 × 34

☐

34 × 28

28 × 56

56 × 47

47 × 64

Champions' Challenge

1) Square each number between 30 and 40. What pattern do you find in the 1s digits of the answers?

2) Do you think this pattern will be the same for the square of numbers between 40 and 50? Why or why not?

I found this:

Have you mastered...?

properties of polygons

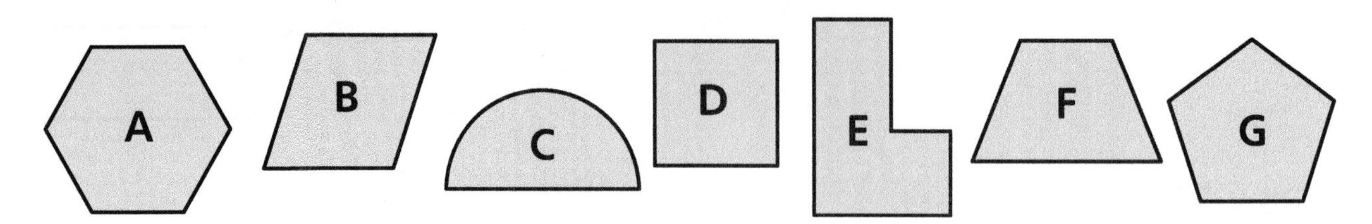

a) List the letters of the shapes that:

are regular polygons ______________

are irregular quadrilaterals ______________

have at least one pair of parallel sides ______________

have at least one pair of perpendicular sides ______________

b) Draw a symmetrical quadrilateral with two obtuse angles and two acute angles.

Champions' Challenge

Write true or false for each statement.

1) A rectangle is a regular polygon. ____________

2) A rectangle is an irregular quadrilateral. ____________

3) A rectangle is a parallelogram. ____________

4) A square is a rectangle. ____________

5) A rectangle is a square. ____________

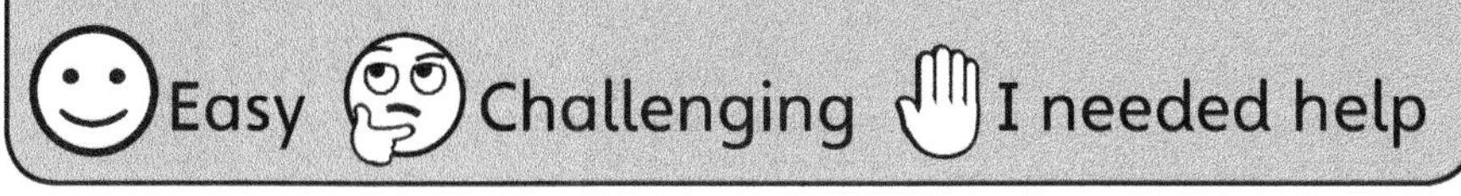

Have you mastered...?

improper fractions, mixed numbers and equivalent fractions

a) Write >, < or = between each pair.

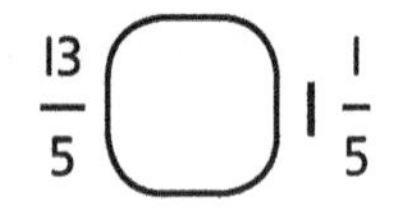

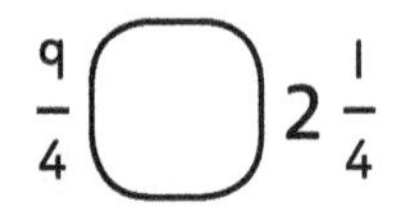

$\frac{11}{8}$ ☐ $1\frac{7}{8}$

$2\frac{1}{7}$ ☐ $\frac{15}{7}$

$\frac{7}{5}$ ☐ $\frac{5}{7}$

b) Sketch a line from 0 to 2 and place the following fractions on it.

$\frac{15}{8}$ $\frac{5}{4}$ $\frac{4}{5}$ $\frac{2}{3}$ $\frac{3}{2}$

c) Complete this sequence. Write each fraction in the simplest way possible.

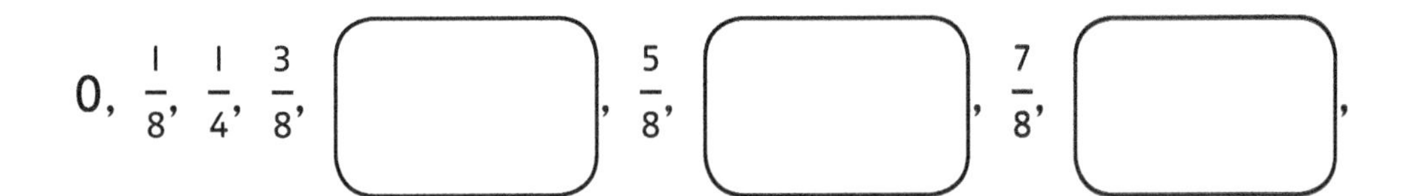

$0, \frac{1}{8}, \frac{1}{4}, \frac{3}{8},$ ☐, $\frac{5}{8},$ ☐, $\frac{7}{8},$ ☐,

$1\frac{1}{8},$ ☐, ☐, $1\frac{1}{2}, 1\frac{5}{8}, 1\frac{3}{4},$ ☐, 2

Champions' Challenge

Write five improper fractions between 4 and 5. Each must have a different denominator.

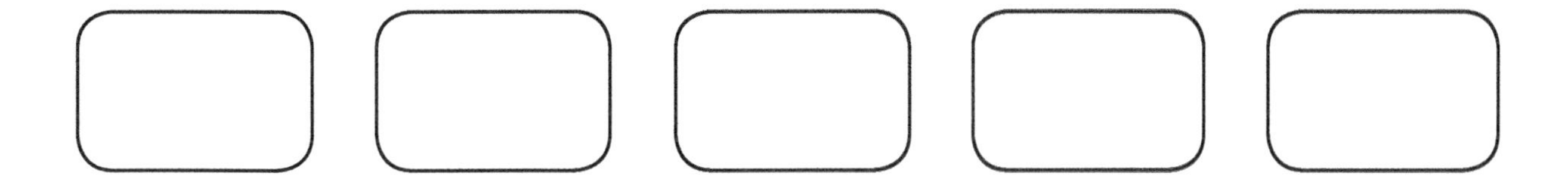

I found this:

 Easy  Challenging  I needed help

Have you mastered...?

subtracting 4-digit numbers and adding more than two numbers

a) Work out the answers to these subtractions. Choose the best way to do each one.

7005 – 4968

6248 – 3526

6400 – 3895

8391 – 4825

b) Solve these additions:

6321 + 2508 + 3543

634 + 15 + 287 + 352

7529 + 5217 + 346

5432 + 58 + 721

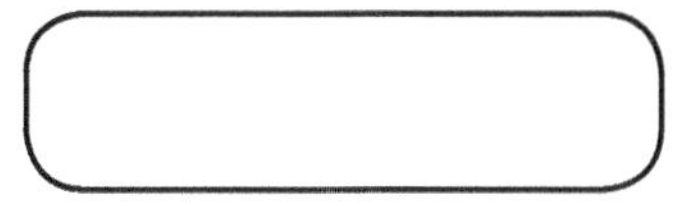

c) A village has 5378 men, 5421 women, 3329 children, 134 dogs and 205 cats. How many people live in the village altogether?

What is the difference between the number of men and the number of women?

Champions' Challenge

Use the digits 0 to 9 to make a 4-digit number and two 3-digit numbers with a total of exactly 9000. No digit must be used more than once!

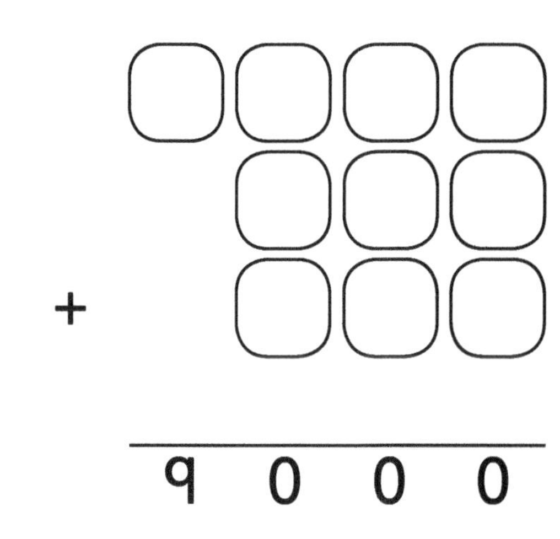

I found this:

 Easy  Challenging  I needed help

Have you mastered...?

solving and checking word problems

Costs at the Funfair

Big Dipper	£3·75
Dodgems	£2·50
Helter Skelter	£2·35
Ghost Train	£2·85
Ice Cream	£1·30
Popcorn	99p
Slush Drink	75p

a) Samara goes on the Big Dipper and the Ghost Train, and she buys a slush drink. How much does she spend?

b) Ahmed has £10. He goes on the Dodgems and the Helter Skelter and buys two ice creams. How much has he got left?

c) Mona has three goes on the Ghost Train and buys some popcorn. How much does she spend?

d) Round each cost and give an approximate total if you had gone on all the rides.

e) Use a different method or an inverse operation to explain how you can check at least one of your answers.

Champions' Challenge

You have got £15 to spend at the funfair. Choose any three rides and any two treats. How much do you have left?

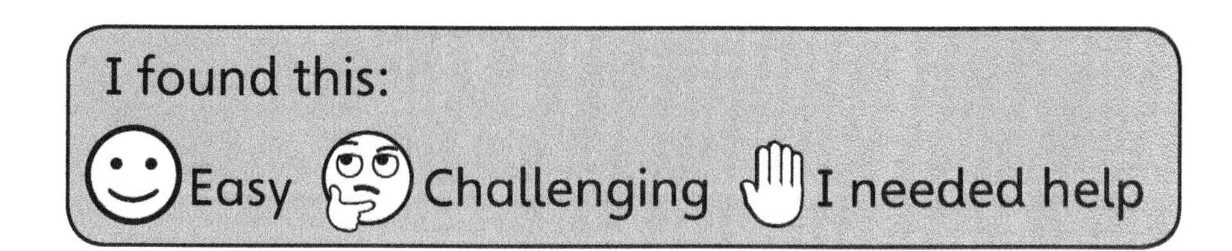

Have you mastered...?

multiplying proper fractions

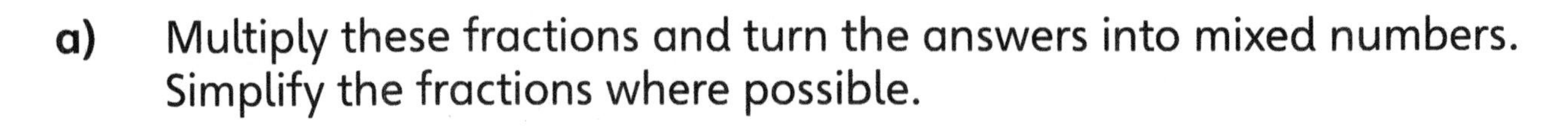

a) Multiply these fractions and turn the answers into mixed numbers. Simplify the fractions where possible.

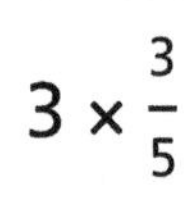

$3 \times \frac{3}{5}$ 

$4 \times \frac{5}{6}$ 

$5 \times \frac{5}{8}$ 

$6 \times \frac{7}{12}$ 

b) 5 friends each eat $\frac{3}{8}$ of a pizza. Altogether, is that more or less than 2 whole pizzas? How do you know?

____

____

Champions' Challenge

1) Layla is working out her $\frac{3}{4}$ times-table. Help her to fill it in.

$1 \times \frac{3}{4} =$ ☐ $2 \times \frac{3}{4} =$ ☐ $3 \times \frac{3}{4} =$ ☐

$4 \times \frac{3}{4} =$ ☐ $5 \times \frac{3}{4} =$ ☐ $6 \times \frac{3}{4} =$ ☐

$7 \times \frac{3}{4} =$ ☐ $8 \times \frac{3}{4} =$ ☐ $9 \times \frac{3}{4} =$ ☐

$10 \times \frac{3}{4} =$ ☐ $11 \times \frac{3}{4} =$ ☐ $12 \times \frac{3}{4} =$ ☐

2) She says that three of the answers are whole numbers. Is she right?

____

____

3) What other patterns can you find?

____

____

4) Work out the $\frac{2}{5}$ times-table up to $10 \times \frac{2}{5}$. How many whole numbers do you think there will be?

I found this:

Have you mastered...?

short multiplication methods

a) Which of these multiplication questions do you think will give an answer closest to 30 000?

6 × 4059   7 × 2383   6 × 6277   8 × 3821

Explain your thinking.

b) Which might give an answer lower than 20 000?

Explain your thinking.

c) Set out and solve each of the multiplications. Was your guess for question **(a)** correct?

Champions' Challenge

1) Which do you think will be the heaviest, 6 parcels each of mass 3452 grams or 8 parcels each of mass 2589 grams?

2) Now work out the total masses. Were you right?

What is the total mass of the heavier set of parcels?

3) If 12 parcels that were all the same size come to the heavier mass in question 2, what is the mass of each parcel?

I found this:

Easy Challenging I needed help

Have you mastered...?

working with 3-place decimals

a) Write the four decimal numbers in each set in order, smallest first.

3·725 3·075 5·715 3·715

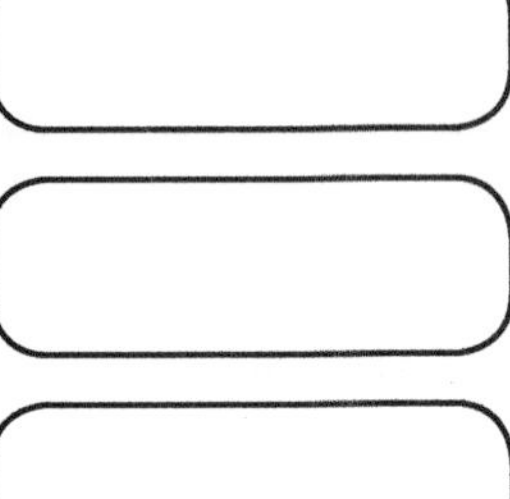

0·549 0·05 0·4 0·059

b) What is the value of the digit 8 in each of these numbers?

0·187 ____________________

3·508 ____________________

18·639 ____________________

2·89 ____________________

c) Solve these calculations:

0·753 × 1000 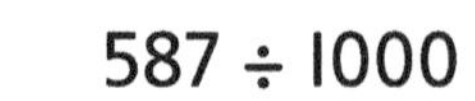

587 ÷ 1000 

6·2 ÷ 100

39·121 × 100

Champions' Challenge

1) Find the number exactly halfway between each of these pairs:

3·17 and 3·18

3·406 and 3·468

0·189 and 0·311

6·73 and 7·24

2) Put these five parcels in order of size, smallest first.

A: 1·7 kg B: 1760 grams C: 1·706 kg D: 1 kg 716 g E: 756 g

3) Write an explanation for a friend about how you solved question 2.

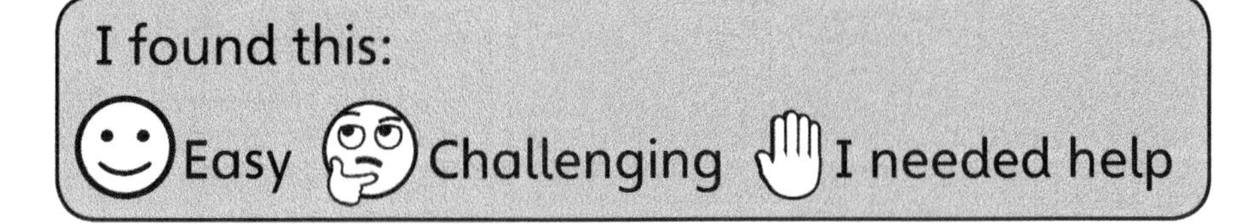

Have you mastered...?

solving problems with negative numbers

a) Zebra Class are counting backwards. What are the next three numbers in each sequence?

8, 6, 4, ___, ___, ___

15, 10, 5, ___, ___, ___

7, 4, 1, ___, ___, ___

b) Write the cities in order, coldest to warmest.

City temperatures on Monday morning	
Glasgow	-1°C
Helsinki	-7°C
London	3°C
Madrid	12°C
Moscow	-11°C
Stockholm	-4°C

______

______

______

______

______

______

c) Find the difference in temperature between:

London and Stockholm

Helsinki and Glasgow

Moscow and Madrid

Champions' Challenge

1) The night-time temperature of each city is 6°C lower than the temperature during the day. Draw up a table showing the night-time temperatures.

2) On Wednesday the temperature of each city is 2·5°C higher than on Monday. Peter says the temperature in Helsinki is ⁻5·5°C, but his teacher says that is wrong. Can you explain why?

___

___

___

What is the temperature in Moscow and Glasgow on Wednesday?

Moscow [ ] Glasgow [ ]

I found this:

Easy Challenging I needed help

Have you mastered...?

working with coordinates in the first two quadrants

Look at the shape on this grid.

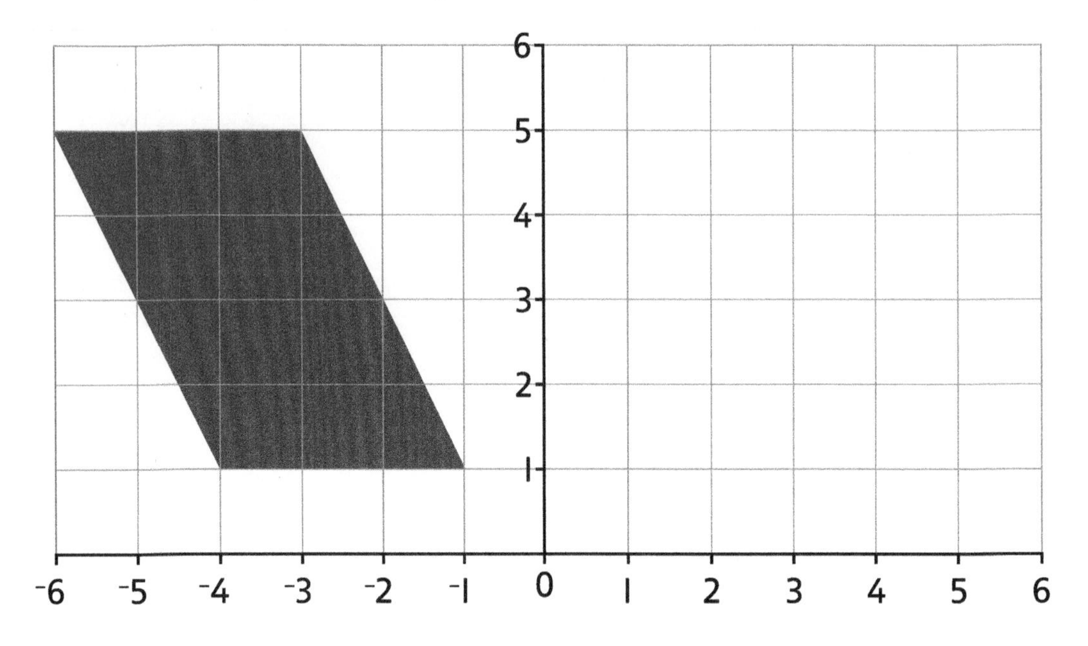

a) What are the coordinates of the corners of the shape?

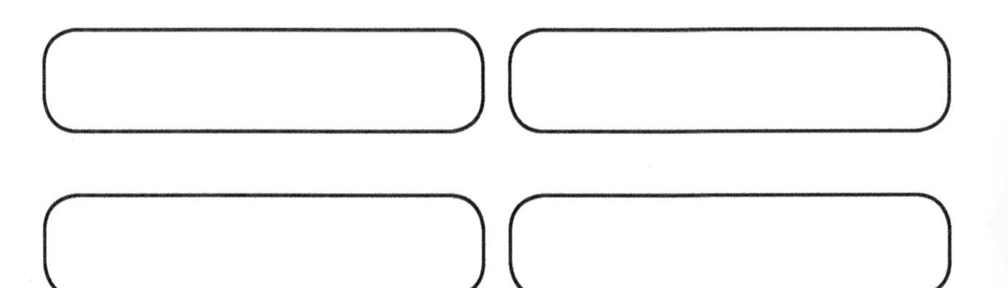

b) If the shape is moved six squares to the right, what will its new coordinates be?

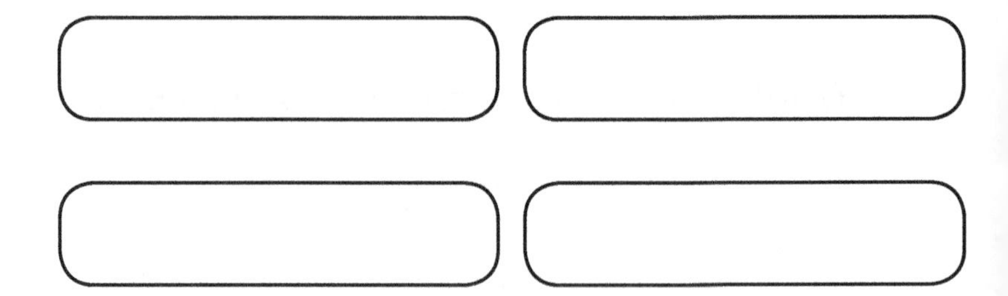

c) Compare the coordinates before and after the move. What do you notice about the y-coordinate in each case?

Why is this?

d) Reflect the shape in the y-axis.

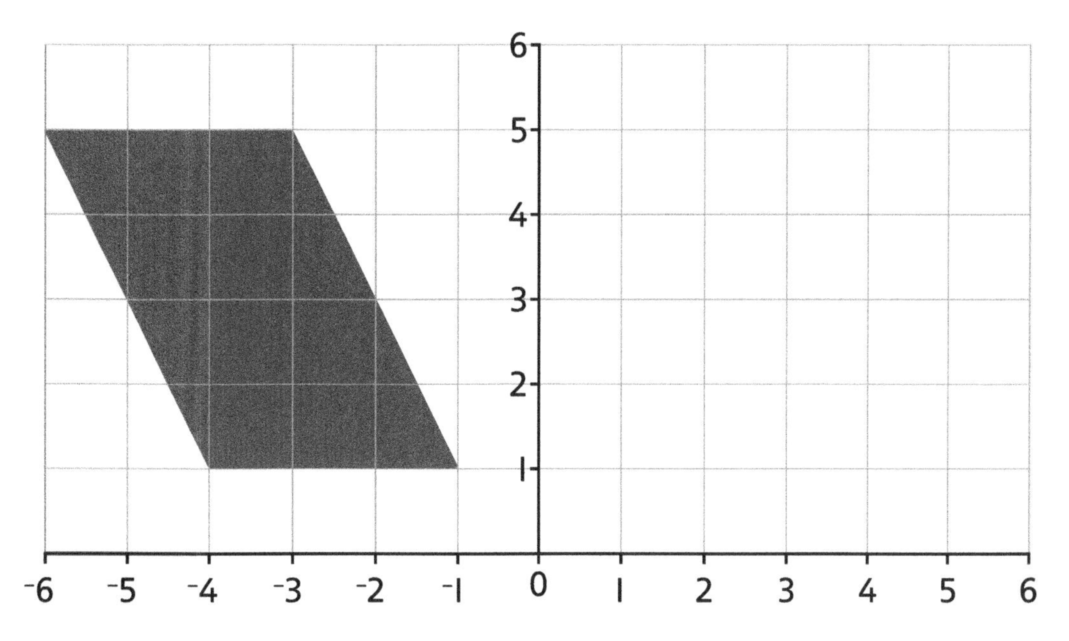

What are its coordinates now?

I found this: Easy Challenging I needed help

Continues on next page

Have you mastered...?

working with coordinates in the first two quadrants

Champions' Challenge

1) On this grid, plot a hexagon in the first quadrant.

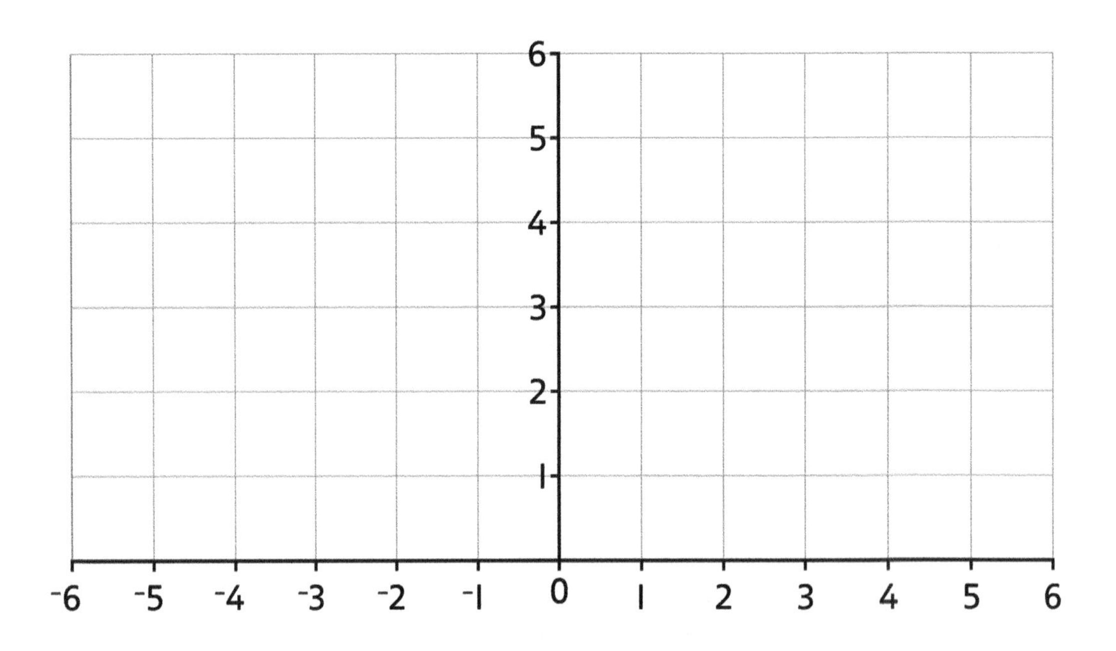

2) What are its coordinates?

3) Imagine that the hexagon is translated (moved) four squares to the left and three squares up.

Without re-drawing it, give its new coordinates.

Explain how you did this.

Have you mastered...?

drawing 2D shapes and identifying 3D shapes from nets

a) Look at these nets. If you cut them out and folded them, what shapes would you get?

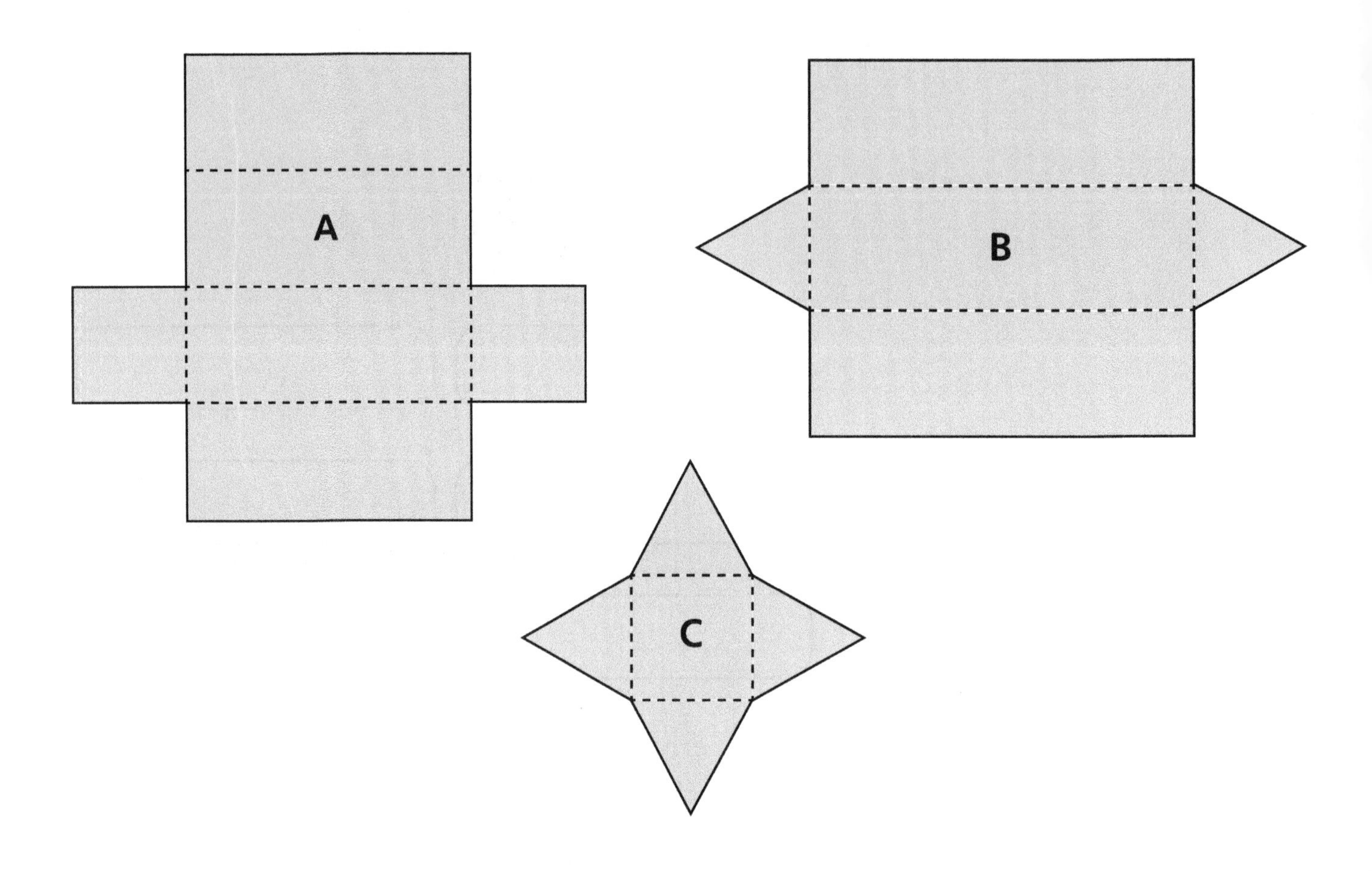

A: ______________________________

B: ______________________________

C: ______________________________

b) Using a ruler and a sharp pencil, draw two different arrangements of six squares that can be folded to make a cube.

I found this:

Easy Challenging I needed help

Continues on next page

drawing 2D shapes and identifying 3D shapes from nets

c) Using a ruler, a pencil and a protractor, draw a triangle with a base 9 cm long, one angle of 65° and one of 20°.

Find the lengths of the other two sides to the nearest cm.

What should the third angle be?

d) How did you know without measuring?

Now check. Were you right?

Champions' Challenge

1) Write some instructions to explain how to draw a parallelogram with sides 11 cm long and 6 cm long, with angles of 130° and 50°.

____

____

____

____

2) Follow your instructions to draw the parallelogram.

Were they clear enough?

____

I found this:

Easy Challenging I needed help

Have you mastered...?

using column methods to solve and check addition and subtraction problems

a) Solve these calculations:

17583 + 26918

78163 – 36576

b) How many more people live in Sedfield than Downsville?

Population of four towns	
Downsville	17903
Gunwich	6675
Pearchester	38745
Sedfield	53721

How can you check your answer?

c) Do you think that the total population of Gunwich, Pearchester and Sedfield is more or less than 100 000?

Now add the populations and see if you were right.

Champions' Challenge

Find two 5-digit numbers that have a total between 75 000 and 80 000 and a difference between 10 000 and 20 000. Your two numbers must use each of the digits 0–9 once only.

I found this:

 Easy  Challenging I needed help

Have you mastered...?

comparing, adding and subtracting fractions

a) Compare, add and find the difference between each pair of fractions. For example:

$\frac{3}{4}$ and $\frac{7}{8}$ $\quad \frac{3}{4} < \frac{7}{8} \left(\text{as } \frac{3}{4} = \frac{6}{8}\right) \quad \frac{3}{4} + \frac{7}{8} = \frac{6}{8} + \frac{7}{8} = \frac{13}{8} = 1\frac{5}{8} \quad \frac{7}{8} - \frac{3}{4} = \frac{1}{8}$

	compare	*add*	*difference*
$\frac{1}{2}$ and $\frac{3}{8}$			
$\frac{7}{10}$ and $\frac{4}{5}$			
$\frac{2}{3}$ and $\frac{7}{9}$			
$\frac{3}{8}$ and $\frac{1}{4}$			
$\frac{5}{6}$ and $\frac{7}{12}$			
$1\frac{1}{3}$ and $1\frac{4}{9}$			

b) Write four fractions between $\frac{1}{2}$ and 1.

Champions' Challenge

1) Write three pairs of fractions, where each fraction has a different denominator. Each pair must have a total of between 1 and $1\frac{1}{2}$.

2) Can you find one pair of fractions with a difference of $\frac{1}{8}$, where each fraction has a different denominator?

Have you mastered...?

short division

a) Solve these divisions. Where there are remainders, write them as fractions.

379 ÷ 3

972 ÷ 8

6342 ÷ 5

3843 ÷ 7

1818 ÷ 4

5236 ÷ 6

9948 ÷ 8

4835 ÷ 9

b) A bakery makes 3250 buns and puts them in packs of 6 buns. How many whole packs can be made?

c) A hotel needs 500 buns. How many packs of 6 do they need to order?

Champions' Challenge

1) Write a division of a 4-digit number by 5 with $\frac{1}{5}$ in the answer.

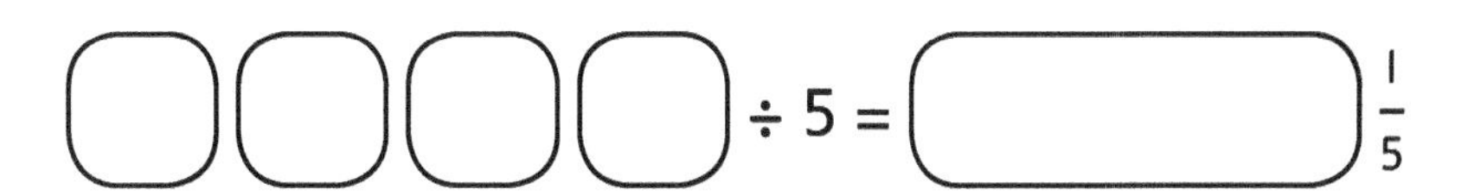

2) Write a division of a 4-digit number by 3 with $\frac{1}{3}$ in the answer.

☐☐☐☐ ÷ 3 = ☐ $\frac{1}{3}$

I found this:

Easy Challenging I needed help

Have you mastered...?

multiplying 3-digit and 4-digit numbers by teens numbers

An online T-shirt shop sold the following numbers of T-shirts last year.

324 robot T-shirts

572 cat T-shirts

1843 spaceship T-shirts

1235 star T-shirts

2412 plain T-shirts

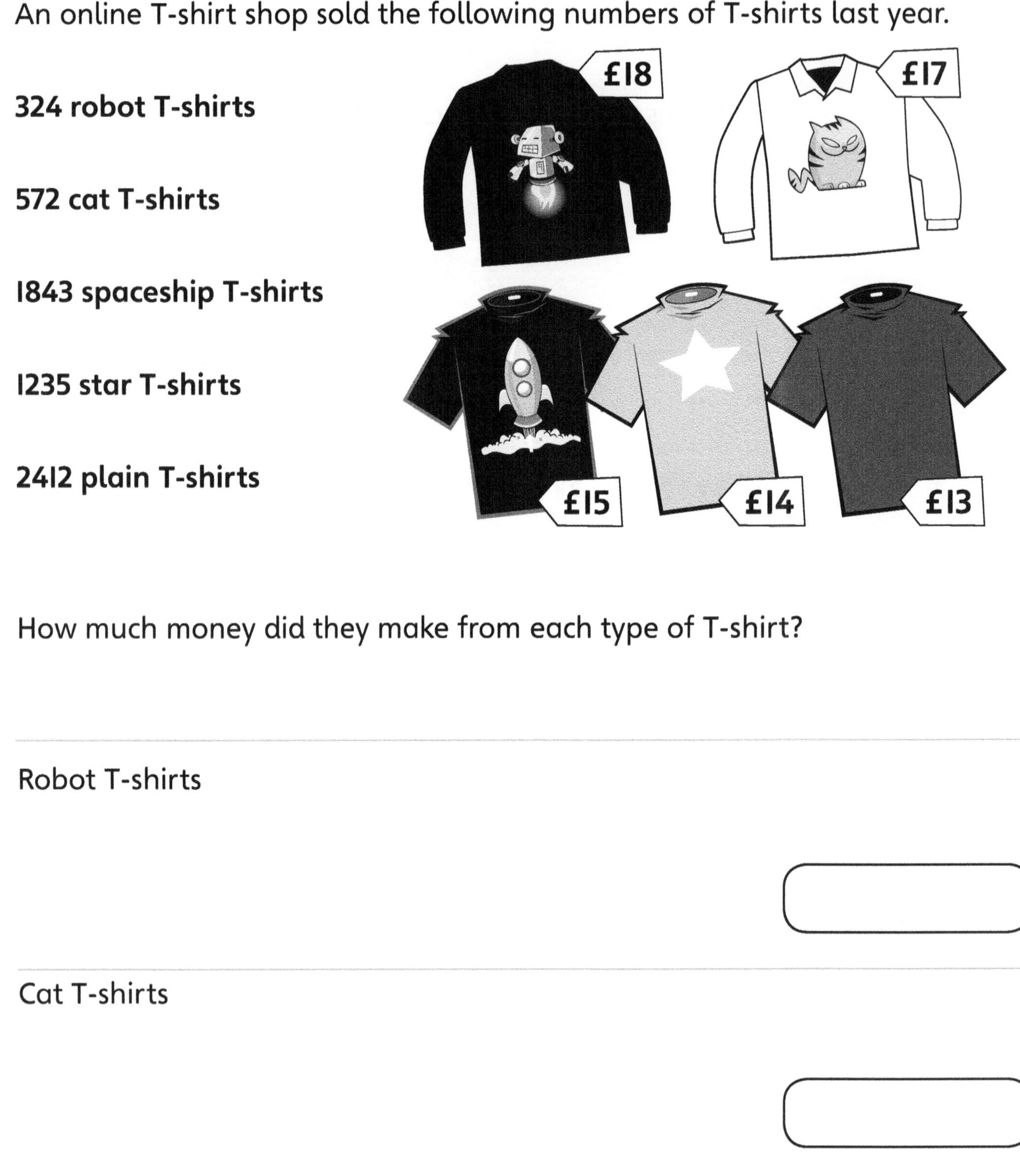

How much money did they make from each type of T-shirt?

Robot T-shirts

Cat T-shirts

Spaceship T-shirts

Star T-shirts

Plain T-shirts

Champions' Challenge

This year, the shop has sold 648 of one of the T-shirts. They have made £9720. Which T-shirt is it?

I found this:

Easy Challenging I needed help

Have you mastered...?

finding areas and perimeters

a) Look at the following shapes. Each small square represents $1\,cm^2$. Work out the area and perimeter of each shape.

A

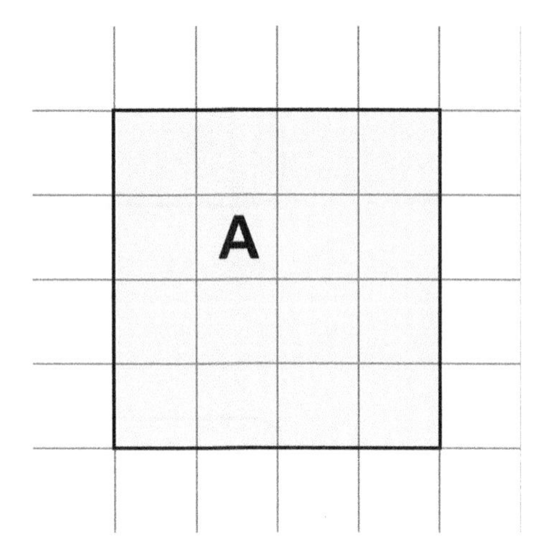

Area: ______________

Perimeter: ______________

B

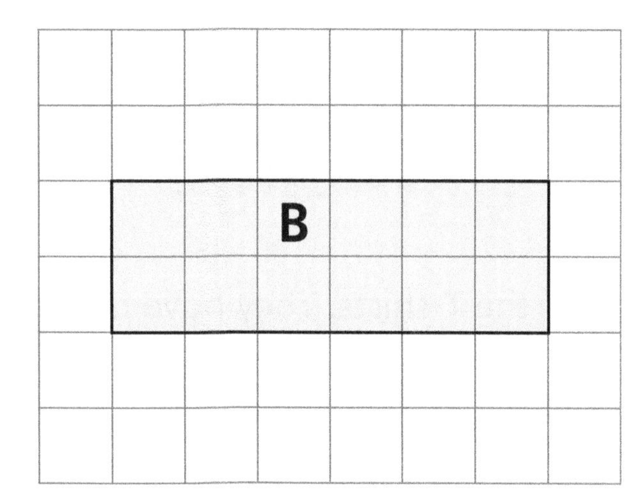

Area: ______________

Perimeter: ______________

C

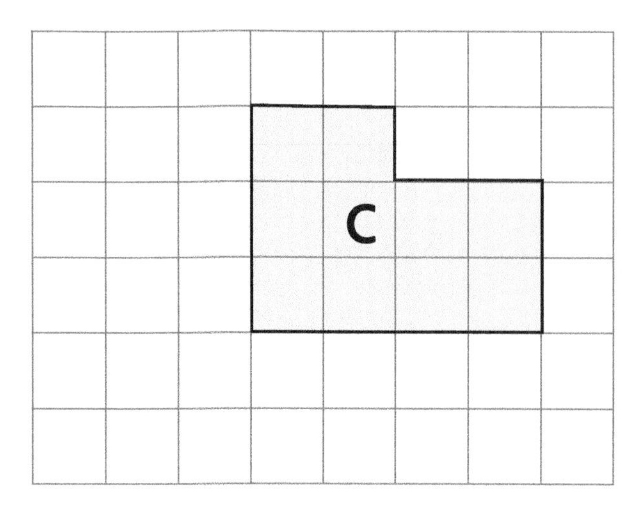

Area: ______________

Perimeter: ______________

b) Draw a leaf on the cm^2 grid with an area of between $10\,cm^2$ and $20\,cm^2$. Find its area to the nearest $\frac{1}{2}\,cm^2$.

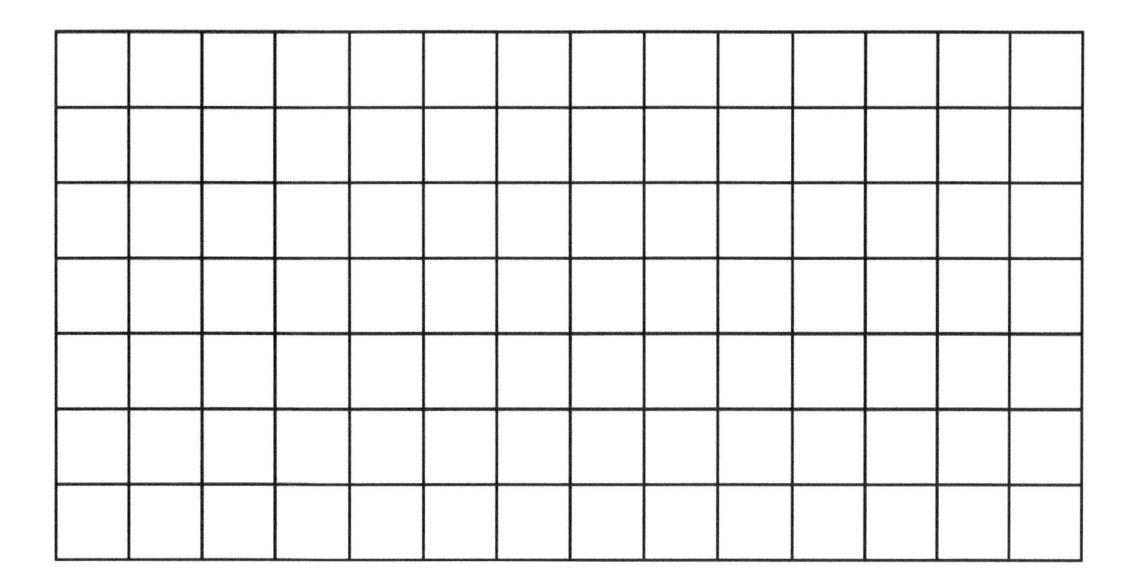

Area: ________________

Champions' Challenge

1) Work out the missing lengths for each of these rectangles.

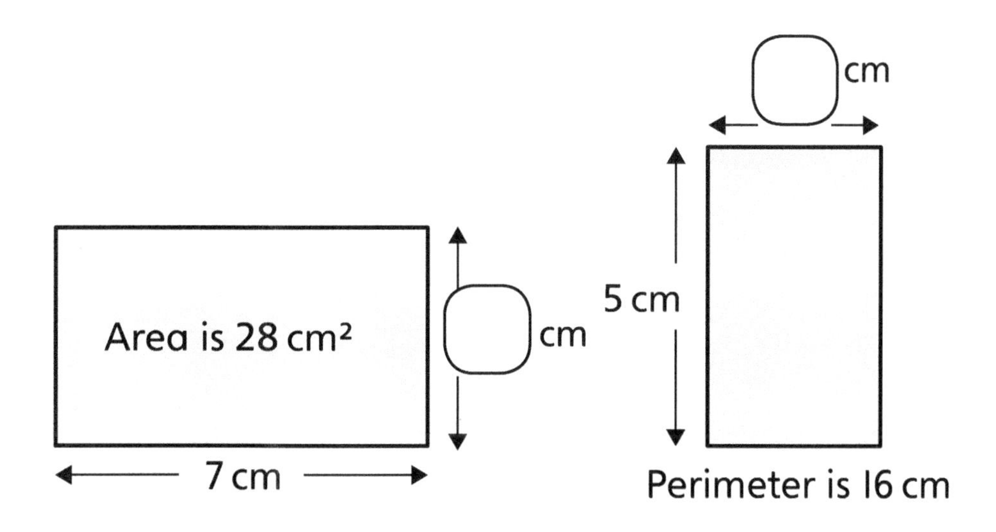

Have you mastered...?

volume and capacity

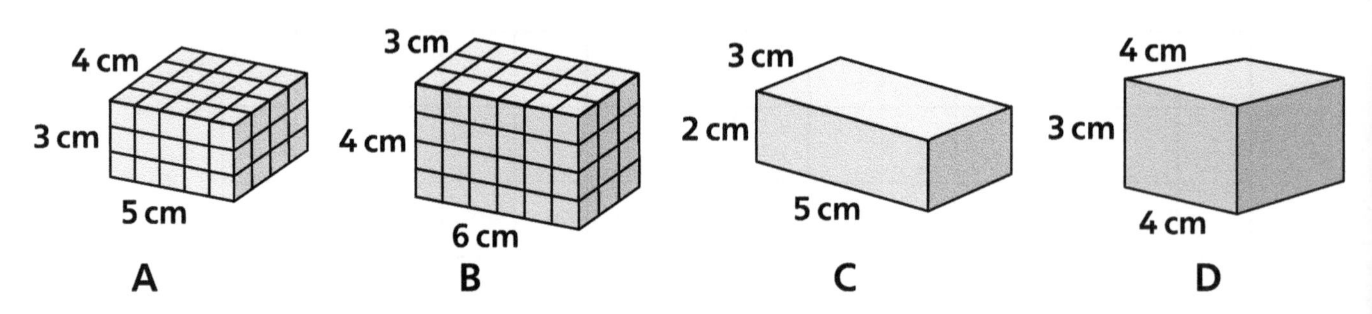

a) Work out the volume of each cuboid.

A

B

C

D

b) If cuboids C and D were hollow, how much water would they hold?

C

D

c) Sketch a cuboid that could hold exactly 36 millilitres of water.

Champions' Challenge

1) If the length of every edge of a cuboid is doubled, does its volume double too?

____

2) Give an example to show whether it does double or does not double.

____

____

____

____

I found this:

Easy Challenging I needed help

Have you mastered...?

fractions, decimals and percentages

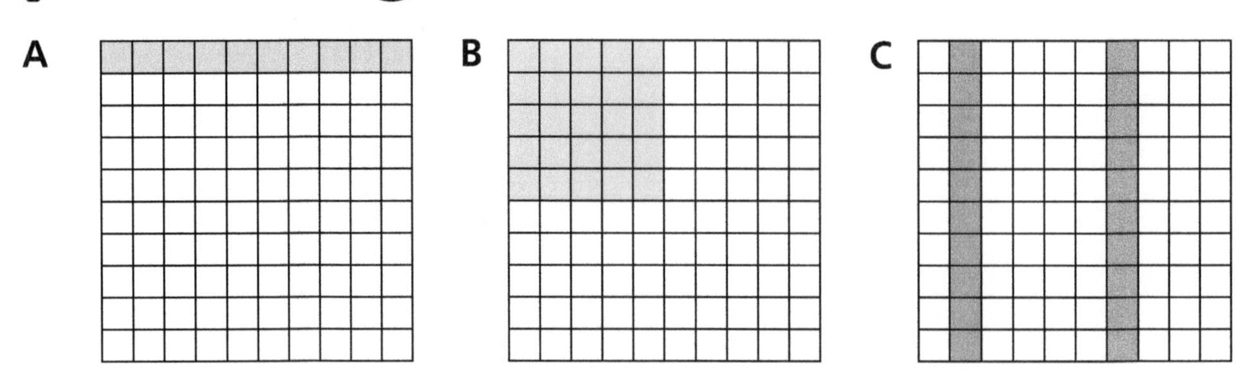

a) Write the percentage that is shaded in each square. Write the percentage as a simplified fraction and as a decimal.

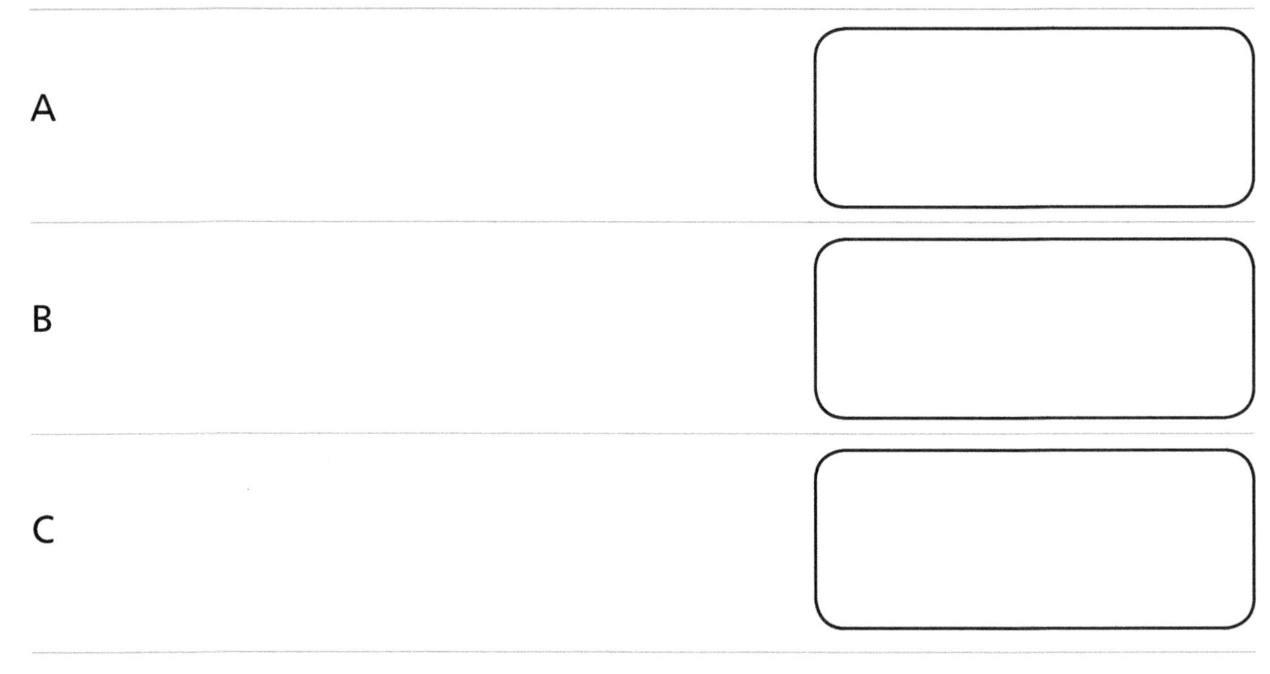

A

B

C

b) Calculate the following percentages of £40:

10%

20%

75%

5%

c) In a class of 32 children, 25% of the children like broccoli. How many children do not like broccoli?

Champions' Challenge

$\frac{4}{7}$ of the 28 children in Class A are girls. 60% of the 30 children in Class B are girls. Which class has more girls in it?

I found this:

 Easy  Challenging  I needed help

Have you mastered...?

reading line graphs

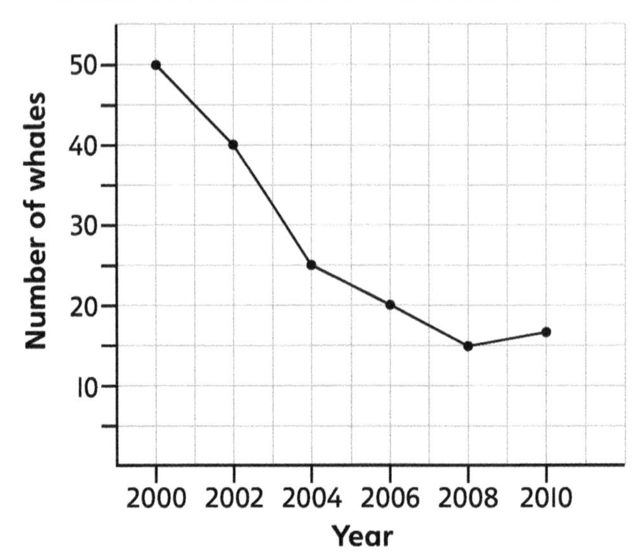

Scientists are concerned that the whale population is declining so they are monitoring the number of whales in an area of ocean.

a) How many whales did they find in 2004?

b) What was the decline in population between 2000 and 2008?

c) Estimate the number of whales in 2001.

d) Were there 12, 15 or 17 whales in 2010?

e) What year do you think caused the scientists the most concern and why?

____

____

f) The scientists were more optimistic in 2010 than in 2006. Why was that?

____

____

Champions' Challenge

If the whale population goes on increasing at the same rate as it did between 2008 and 2010, how long will it take for the whale population to get back to the level it was in the year 2000?

____

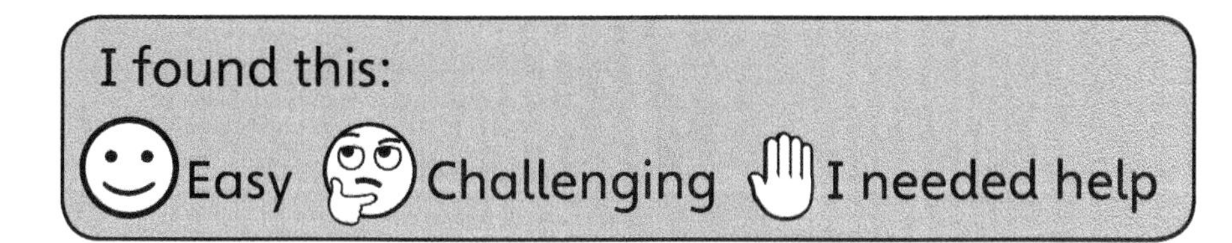

Have you mastered...?

solving problems involving scaling or rate

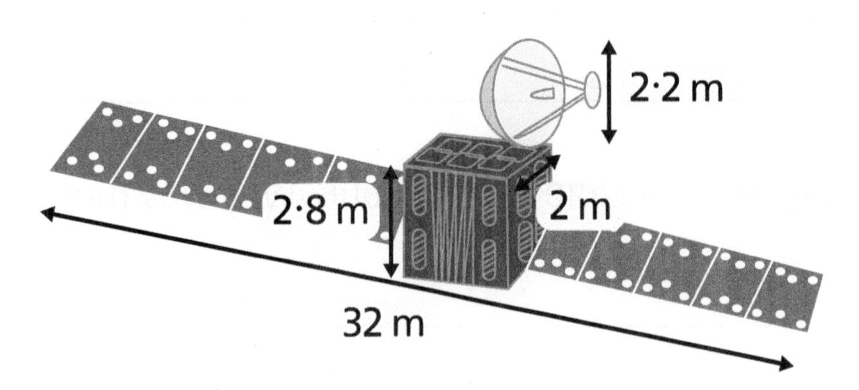

a) Brian is making a scale model of the Rosetta orbiter. It needs to be $\frac{1}{4}$ of the size of the actual orbiter. Work out what each dimension needs to be.

Box height ______________

Box depth ______________

Dish height ______________

Wingspan ______________

b) If you have a resting heart rate of 70 beats per minute, how many times will your heart beat in one hour if you stay still?

____

c) If you walk at a rate of 5 kilometres an hour, how long would it take you to walk 20 kilometres?

____

d) If you drink 2 litres a day, how much will you drink in a year?

____

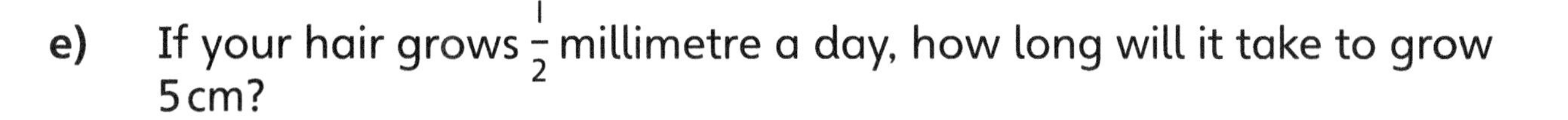

e) If your hair grows $\frac{1}{2}$ millimetre a day, how long will it take to grow 5 cm?

____

Champions' Challenge

Brian wants to make a model of the Rosetta orbiter that would fit on a school desk. What fraction of the original size do you think the model should be?

What would the new wingspan be?

____

I found this:

 Easy  Challenging I needed help

Date: ____________

Thoughts on my learning

As we learn about a new topic in maths, we do lots of thinking! As you are working through a topic, stop and spend some time thinking about what you are learning.

Record some of your thoughts below. Use these sentence starters to help you.

I know… because

I think… because

I know… so I also know

I agree with… because

I disagree with… because

I wonder if…

Date: ________________

Learning from each other

Did you know that we can learn a lot from each other? Together, you and your classmates can help each other understand maths by discussing and explaining ideas.

Think about how your classmates have helped you in your maths learning and how you have helped them.

How have you helped your classmates?

How have your classmates helped you?

Date: ______________

Maths connections

Many of the different areas of maths overlap with each other. For example, if you are converting 160 cm to metres, this involves your skills and knowledge in measurements, decimals, division and place value.

What connections have you spotted between different areas of maths? What did you notice about them?

Date: ____________

Asking questions

You might have heard of the phrase “there is no such thing as a silly question”. This is definitely true when it comes to maths! Asking questions is a really important skill.

Think about the different questions you have asked during your maths learning. Why were these questions important?

Questions I have asked	Why they were important

Date: ______________

My methods

There are lots of different ways to explain maths. You can use different methods and strategies to work out an answer and to help explain your understanding.

Choose one area of maths that you have been learning about. Record some of the different methods and strategies you used during your learning.

Date: ____________________

Reflection

At the end of a topic, stop and reflect on what you have learnt.

What do you understand now that you did not before? Give examples.

What have you got better at? How do you know?

What is the most interesting thing you found out? Give an example.

Is there anything else about this topic you would like to find out more about?

My Mastery

Colour a circle for each skill to show how you feel about it now.

Mastery Checkpoint	Have you mastered...?	More help!	I think I'm OK	I'm the master!	Date
Checkpoint 1 pages 4–5	Place value	○	○	○	
Checkpoint 2 pages 6–7	Mental and written addition	○	○	○	
Checkpoint 3 pages 8–9	The 24-hour clock	○	○	○	
Checkpoint 4 pages 10–11	Factors	○	○	○	
Checkpoint 5 pages 12–13	Mental and written division	○	○	○	
Checkpoint 6 pages 14–15	Angles	○	○	○	
Checkpoint 7 pages 16–17	Ordering numbers with two decimal places	○	○	○	

Colour a circle for each skill to show how you feel about it now.

Mastery Checkpoint	Have you mastered...?	More help!	I think I'm OK	I'm the master!	Date
Checkpoint 8 pages 18–19	Equivalent fractions				
Checkpoint 9 pages 20–21	Mental and written subtraction				
Checkpoint 10 pages 22–23	Mental and written multiplication				
Checkpoint 11 pages 24–25	Place value in 6-digit numbers				
Checkpoint 12 pages 26–27	Numbers with two decimal places				
Checkpoint 13 pages 28–29	Solving word problems involving measures				
Checkpoint 14 pages 30–31	Mental addition and subtraction of large numbers				

My Mastery

Colour a circle for each skill to show how you feel about it now.

Mastery Checkpoint	Have you mastered...?	More help!	I think I'm OK	I'm the master!	Date
Checkpoint 15 pages 32–33	Factors, primes, squares and mental multiplication and division	○	○	○	
Checkpoint 16 pages 34–35	Triangles, including their angles	○	○	○	
Checkpoint 17 pages 36–37	Converting measures	○	○	○	
Checkpoint 18 pages 38–39	Adding and subtracting decimals	○	○	○	
Checkpoint 19 pages 40–41	Short division	○	○	○	
Checkpoint 20 pages 42–43	Finding fractions of amounts	○	○	○	
Checkpoint 21 pages 44–45	Multiplying pairs of 2-digit numbers and 3-digit numbers by 1-digit numbers	○	○	○	

Colour a circle for each skill to show how you feel about it now.

Mastery Checkpoint	Have you mastered...?	More help!	I think I'm OK	I'm the master!	Date
Checkpoint 22 pages 46–47	Properties of polygons				
Checkpoint 23 pages 48–49	Improper fractions, mixed numbers and equivalent fractions				
Checkpoint 24 pages 50–51	Subtracting 4-digit numbers and adding more than two numbers				
Checkpoint 25 pages 52–53	Solving and checking word problems				
Checkpoint 26 pages 54–55	Multiplying proper fractions				
Checkpoint 27 pages 56–57	Short multiplication methods				
Checkpoint 28 pages 58–59	Working with 3-place decimals				

My Mastery

Colour a circle for each skill to show how you feel about it now.

Mastery Checkpoint	Have you mastered...?	More help!	I think I'm OK	I'm the master!	Date
Checkpoint 29 pages 60–61	Solving problems with negative numbers	○	○	○	
Checkpoint 30 pages 62–65	Working with coordinates in the first two quadrants	○	○	○	
Checkpoint 31 pages 66–69	Drawing 2D shapes and identifying 3D shapes from nets	○	○	○	
Checkpoint 32 pages 70–71	Using column methods to solve and check addition and subtraction problems	○	○	○	
Checkpoint 33 pages 72–73	Comparing, adding and subtracting fractions	○	○	○	
Checkpoint 34 pages 74–75	Short division	○	○	○	
Checkpoint 35 pages 76–77	Multiplying 3-digit and 4-digit numbers by teens numbers	○	○	○	

Colour a circle for each skill to show how you feel about it now.

Mastery Checkpoint	Have you mastered...?	More help!	I think I'm OK	I'm the master!	Date
Checkpoint 36 pages 78–79	Finding areas and perimeters				
Checkpoint 37 pages 80–81	Volume and capacity				
Checkpoint 38 pages 82–83	Fractions, decimals and percentages				
Checkpoint 39 pages 84–85	Reading line graphs				
Checkpoint 40 pages 86–87	Solving problems involving scaling or rate				

Checkpoints ordered by curriculum domain

*These Checkpoints fall under more than one domain.